SITE SECTIONS & DETAILS

A Reference Guide to Site Construction Details

SITE SECTIONS
& DETAILS

A Reference Guide to Site Construction Details

David J. Ciaccio

VNR   Van Nostrand Reinhold Company

Copyright © 1984 by Van Nostrand Reinhold Company
Inc.
Library of Congress Catalog Card Number 84-5095
ISBN 0-442-21617-3
ISBN 0-442-23522-4

Printed in the United States of America
Designed by David J. Ciaccio

Published by Van Nostrand Reinhold Company Inc.
135 West 50th Street
New York, New York 10020

Van Nostrand Reinhold Company Limited
Molly Millars Lane
Wokingham, Berkshire RG11 2PY, England

Van Nostrand Reinhold
480 La Trobe Street
Melbourne, Victoria 3000, Australia

Macmillan of Canada
Division of Gage Publishing Limited
164 Commander Boulevard
Agincourt, Ontario M1S 3C7, Canada

16 15 14 13 12 11 10 9 8 7 6 5 4 3 2 1

Library of Congress Cataloging in Publication Data

Ciaccio, David J., 1952-
    Site sections & details.
    Includes index.
    1.Building—Details—Drawings.   2. Building sites.
I. Title.   II. Title: Site sections and details.
TH2031.C54 1984   690   84-5095
ISBN 0-442-21617-3
ISBN 0-442-23522-4

CONTENTS

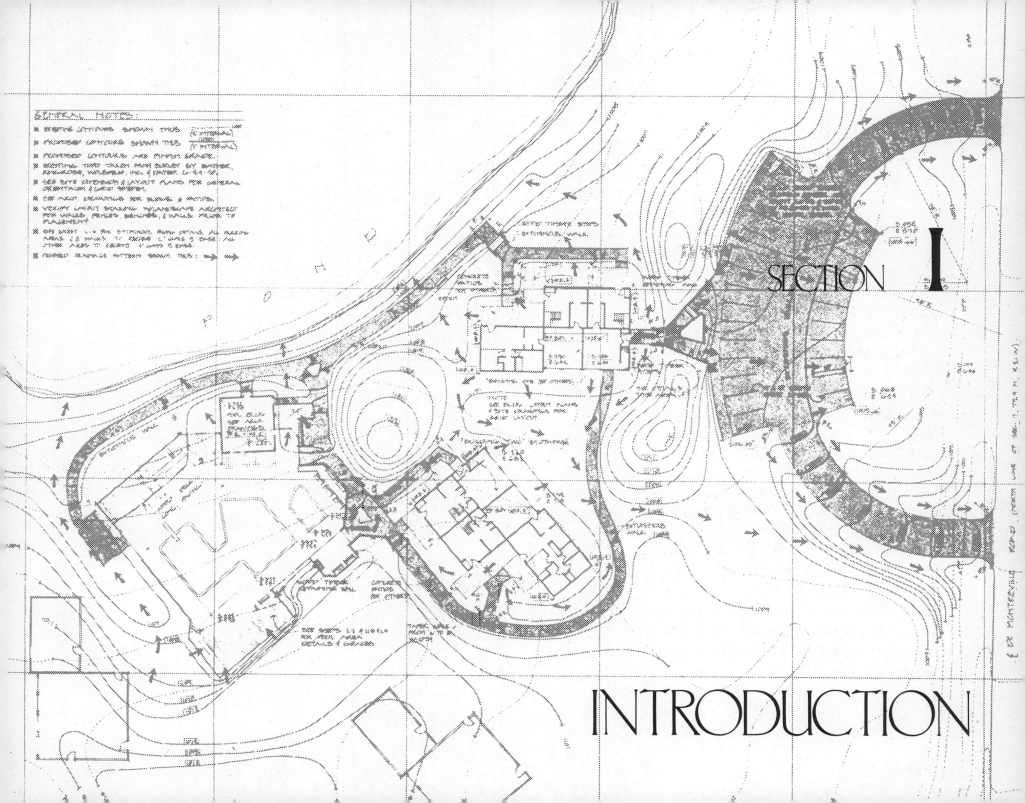

SECTION I

INTRODUCTION

This book is meant to enable profession-
als and students who are involved in the
design and construction of site improve-
ment projects to review and reference
detailing techniques that have been
used in other projects throughout the
country. Technical and graphic illustra-
tions are provided for numerous construction details, which may be incor-
porated into future projects in order to
expedite the production of detail drawings.

Each detail incorporates proven construction techniques while remaining
cognizant of costs. Since the details pre-
sented here were prepared for specific
project use—and therefore in consid-
eration of specific governing codes and
ordinances, site concerns and environ-
mental constraints—the use of any detailing concept illustrated herein should
be preceded by a thorough review of
similar considerations applied to the
project under study.

To my wife Cathryn and son Michael for their love, support and perseverance throughout the past year ... all those future plans and dreams are coming true ...

And to my father and mother who encouraged me to follow those dreams so many years ago ...

3

Special thanks to my partner Loran
Galpin for use of his superior projects
throughout the midwest . . .

Special recognition to Jack Boesch
for contributing his creativity to the
design of the cover . . . and to Dolores
Jurgensen for her assistance in graphic presentation . . .

4

SECTION 2

GRADING & DRAINAGE

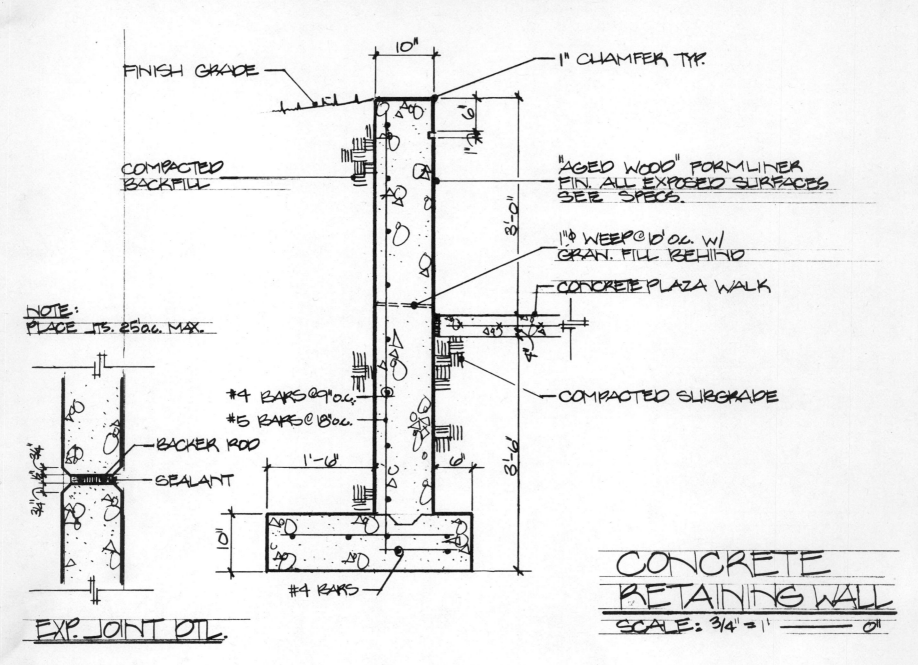

FINISH GRADE

10"

1" CHAMFER TYP.

COMPACTED BACKFILL

"AGED WOOD" FORM LINER FIN. ALL EXPOSED SURFACES SEE SPECS.

3'-0"

1"Ø WEEP @ 10' O.C. W/ GRAN. FILL BEHIND

CONCRETE PLAZA WALK

COMPACTED SUBGRADE

NOTE:
PLACE JTS. 25' O.C. MAX.

BACKER ROD

SEALANT

#4 BARS @ 9" O.C.

#5 BARS @ 18" O.C.

1'-6"

6"

3'-6"

10"

#4 BARS

EXP. JOINT DTL.

CONCRETE RETAINING WALL

SCALE: 3/4" = 1'   0"

6

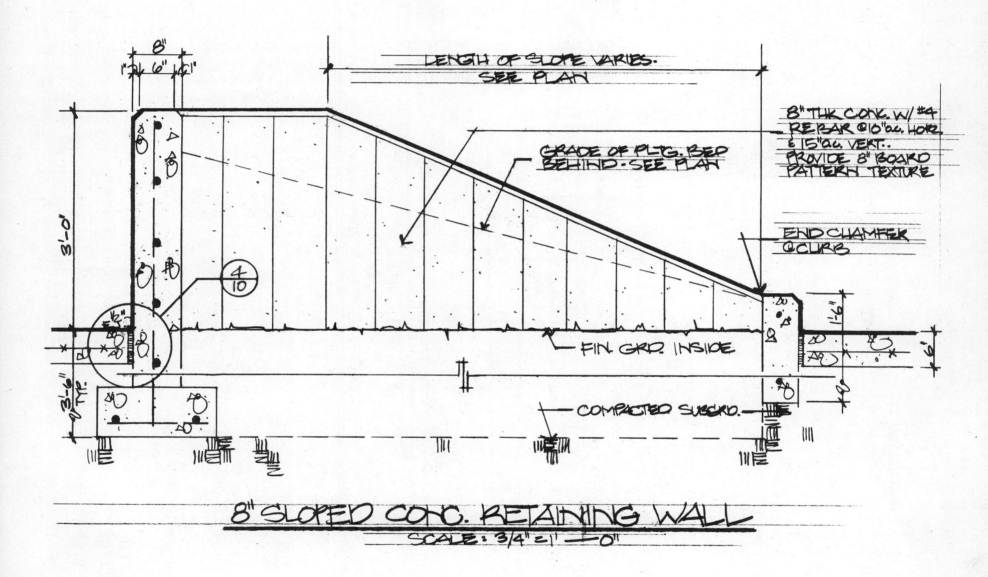

LENGTH OF SLOPE VARIES.
SEE PLAN

8" THK. CONC. W/ #4
REBAR @10"O.C. HORZ.
& 15"O.C. VERT..
PROVIDE 8" BOARD
PATTERN TEXTURE

GRADE OF PLTG. BED
BEHIND. SEE PLAN

END CHAMFER
@ CURB

FIN. GRD. INSIDE

COMPACTED SUBGRD.

8"
6"

3'-0"

4/10

3'-6" TYP.

8" SLOPED CONC. RETAINING WALL
SCALE: 3/4"=1'—0"

7

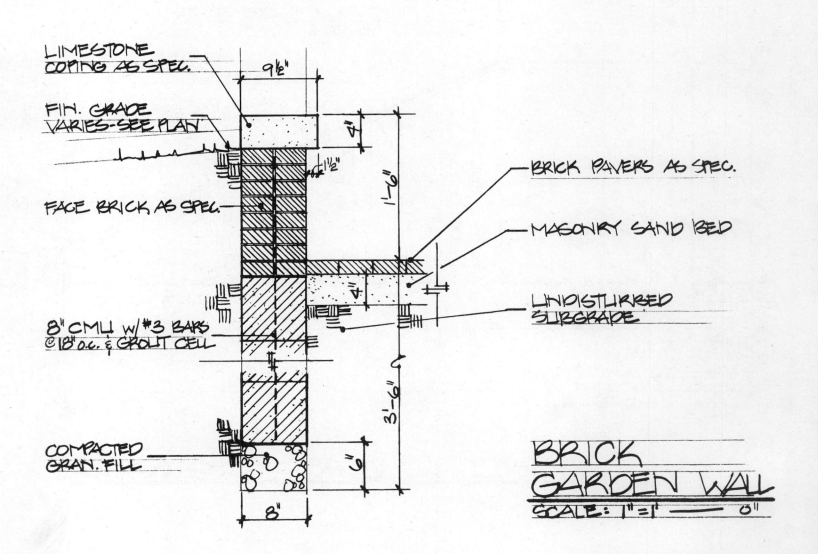

LIMESTONE
COPING AS SPEC.

FIN. GRADE
VARIES-SEE PLAN

FACE BRICK AS SPEC.

8" CMU W/ #3 BARS
@ 18" O.C. & GROUT CELL

COMPACTED
GRAN. FILL

BRICK PAVERS AS SPEC.

MASONRY SAND BED

UNDISTURBED
SUBGRADE

9½"

2"

1½"

1'-6"

4"

3'-6"

6"

8"

BRICK
GARDEN WALL
SCALE: 1"=1'—— 0"

8

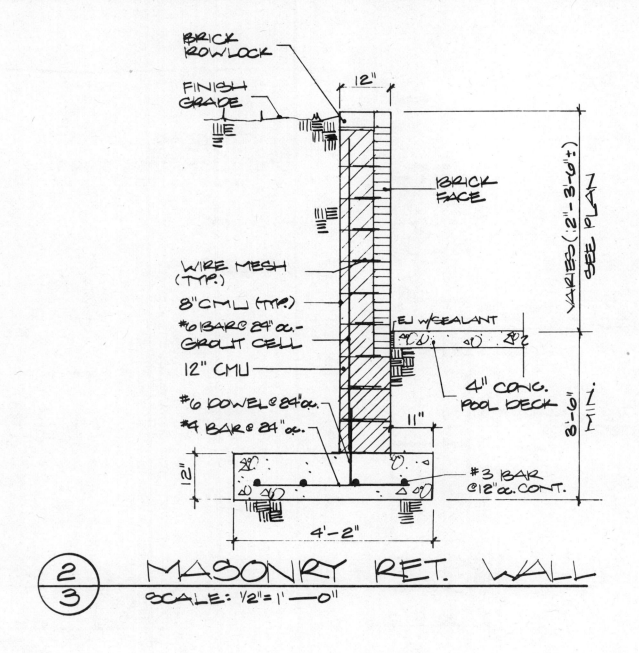

BRICK
ROWLOCK

FINISH
GRADE

12"

BRICK
FACE

WIRE MESH
(TYP.)

8" CMU (TYP.)

#6 BAR @ 24" o.c.-
GROUT CELL

12" CMU

EJ W/SEALANT

4" CONC.
POOL DECK

#6 DOWEL @ 24" o.c.

#4 BAR @ 24" o.c.

11"

#3 BAR
@12" o.c. CONT.

12"

4'-2"

VARIES (12'-3'-6"±)
SEE PLAN

8'-6"
MIN.

2/3 MASONRY RET. WALL
SCALE: 1/2"=1'-0"

9

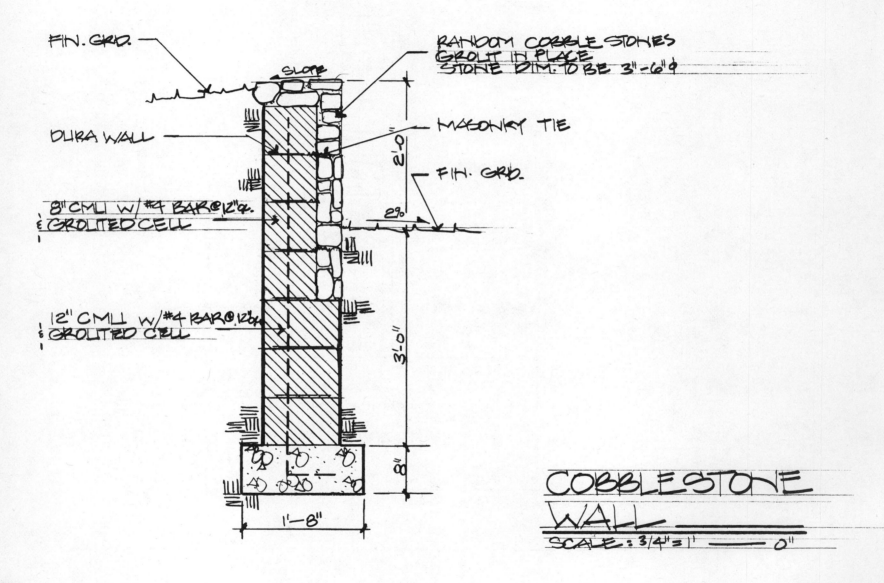

FIN. GRD.

RANDOM COBBLE STONES
GROUT IN PLACE
STONE DIM. TO BE 3"-6" φ

SLOPE

DURA WALL

MASONRY TIE

8" CMU W/ #4 BAR@12"o.c.
& GROUTED CELL

FIN. GRD.

2°

2'-0"

12" CMU W/ #4 BAR@12"o.c.
& GROUTED CELL

3'-0"

8"

1'-8"

COBBLESTONE WALL

SCALE: 3/4" = 1' — 0"

10

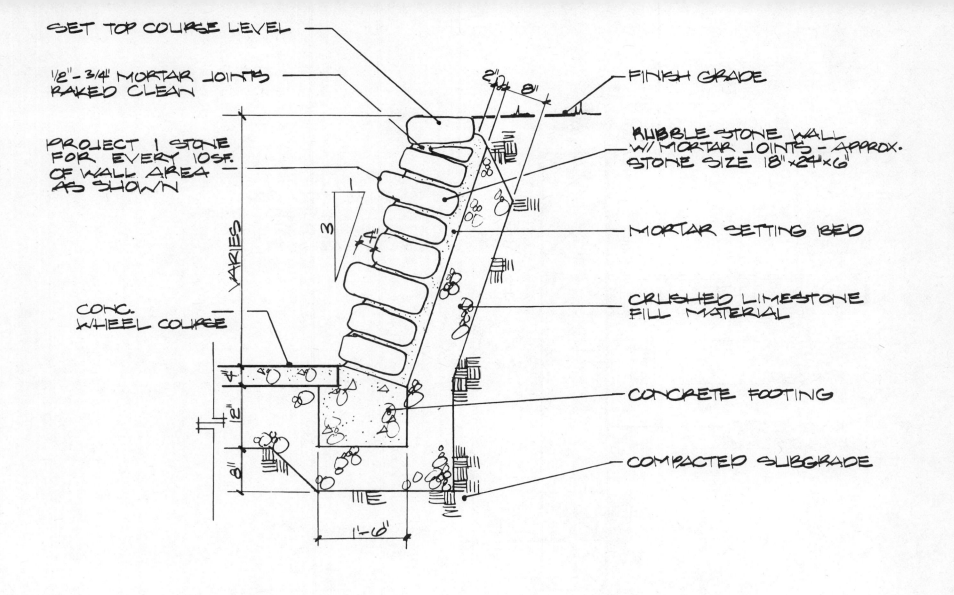

SET TOP COURSE LEVEL

1/2"-3/4" MORTAR JOINTS RAKED CLEAN

PROJECT 1 STONE FOR EVERY 10 S.F. OF WALL AREA AS SHOWN

CONC. WHEEL COURSE

VARIES

3

4"

4"

12"

8"

1'-6"

2" 8"

FINISH GRADE

RUBBLE STONE WALL W/ MORTAR JOINTS - APPROX. STONE SIZE 18"x24"x6"

MORTAR SETTING BED

CRUSHED LIMESTONE FILL MATERIAL

CONCRETE FOOTING

COMPACTED SUBGRADE

5/5 STONE RETAINING WALL
NO SCALE

11

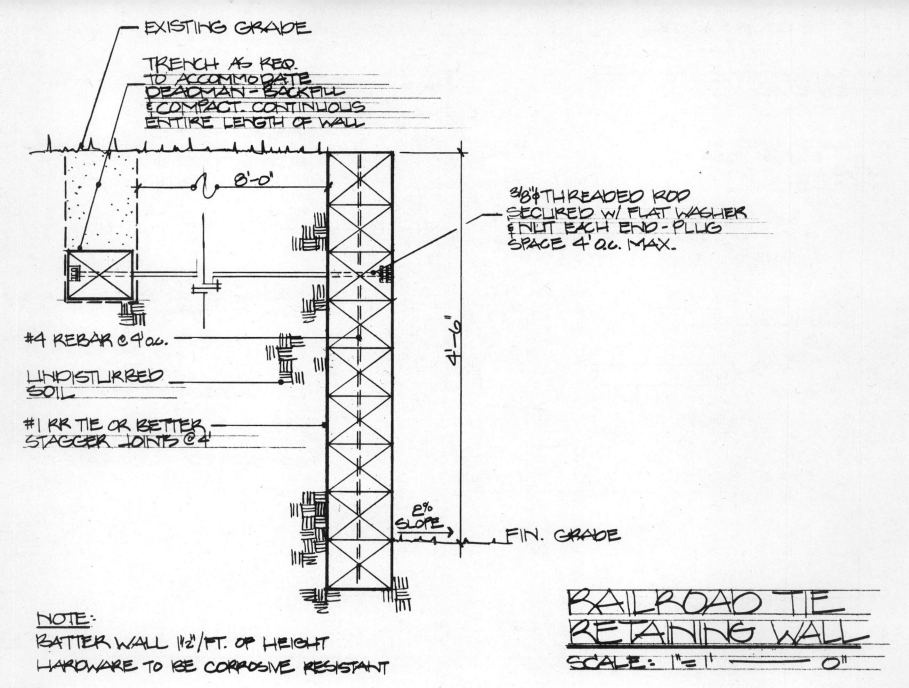

EXISTING GRADE

TRENCH AS REQ.
TO ACCOMMODATE
DEADMAN-BACKFILL
& COMPACT. CONTINUOUS
ENTIRE LENGTH OF WALL

8'-0"

3/8"⌀ THREADED ROD
SECURED w/ FLAT WASHER
& NUT EACH END - PLUG
SPACE 4' O.C. MAX.

4'-0"

#4 REBAR @ 4' O.C.

UNDISTURBED
SOIL

#1 RR TIE OR BETTER
STAGGER JOINTS @ 4'

2% SLOPE

FIN. GRADE

NOTE:
BATTER WALL 1 1/2"/FT. OF HEIGHT
HARDWARE TO BE CORROSIVE RESISTANT

RAILROAD TIE
RETAINING WALL
SCALE: 1" = 1'———— 0"

12

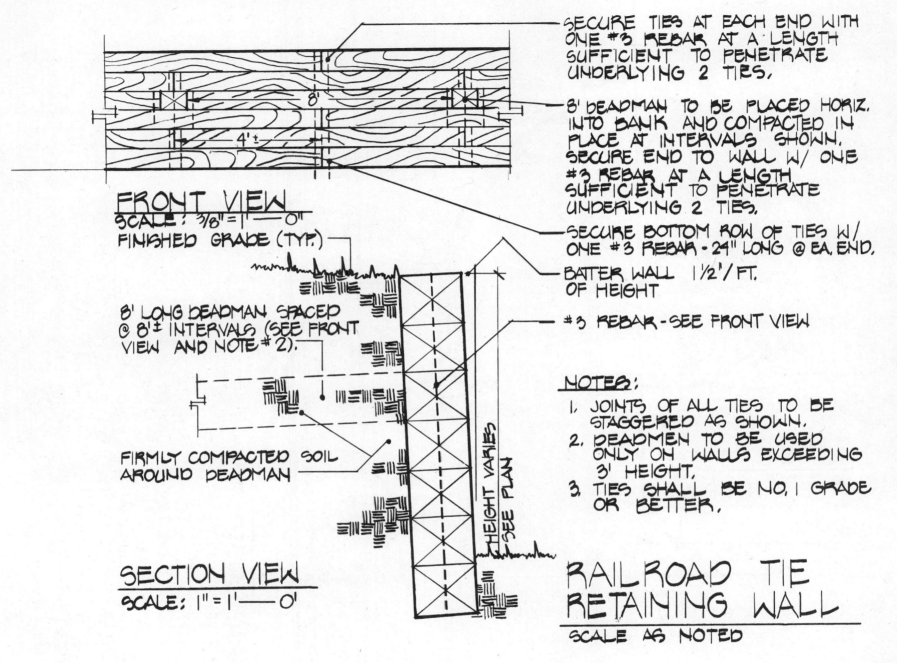

FRONT VIEW
SCALE: 3/8" = 1' — 0"

SECURE TIES AT EACH END WITH ONE #3 REBAR AT A LENGTH SUFFICIENT TO PENETRATE UNDERLYING 2 TIES.

8' DEADMAN TO BE PLACED HORIZ. INTO BANK AND COMPACTED IN PLACE AT INTERVALS SHOWN. SECURE END TO WALL W/ ONE #3 REBAR AT A LENGTH SUFFICIENT TO PENETRATE UNDERLYING 2 TIES.

SECURE BOTTOM ROW OF TIES W/ ONE #3 REBAR - 24" LONG @ EA. END.

BATTER WALL 1 1/2"/ FT. OF HEIGHT

#3 REBAR - SEE FRONT VIEW

FINISHED GRADE (TYP.)

8' LONG DEADMAN SPACED @ 8'± INTERVALS (SEE FRONT VIEW AND NOTE #2).

FIRMLY COMPACTED SOIL AROUND DEADMAN

HEIGHT VARIES SEE PLAN

SECTION VIEW
SCALE: 1" = 1' — 0'

NOTES:
1. JOINTS OF ALL TIES TO BE STAGGERED AS SHOWN.
2. DEADMEN TO BE USED ONLY ON WALLS EXCEEDING 3' HEIGHT.
3. TIES SHALL BE NO. 1 GRADE OR BETTER.

RAILROAD TIE RETAINING WALL
SCALE AS NOTED

13

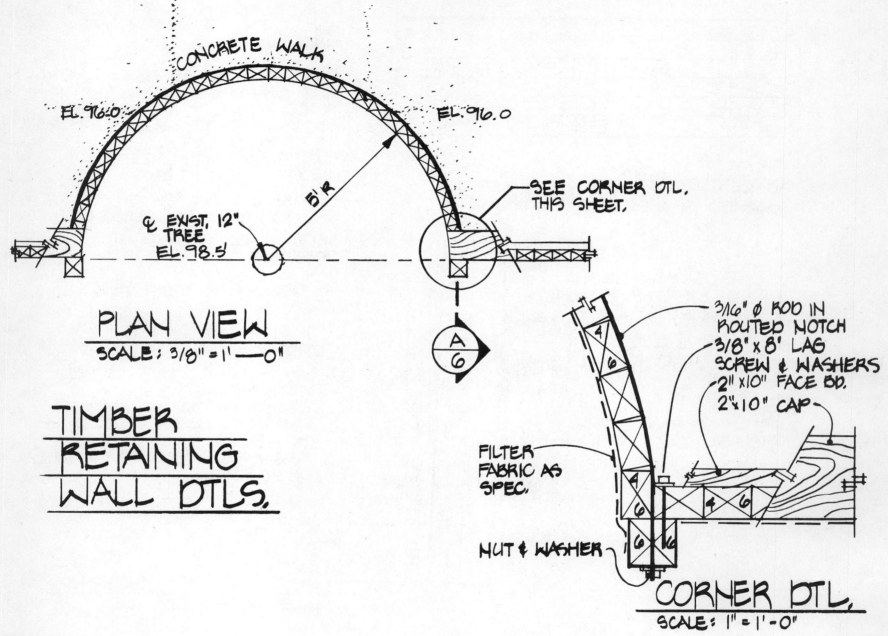

CONCRETE WALK

EL. 96.0   EL. 96.0

5' R

SEE CORNER DTL.
THIS SHEET.

¢ EXIST. 12"
TREE
EL. 98.5'

PLAN VIEW
SCALE: 3/8" = 1'—0"

A
6

TIMBER
RETAINING
WALL DTLS.

3/16" Ø ROD IN
ROUTED NOTCH
3/8" x 8" LAG
SCREW & WASHERS
2" x 10" FACE BD.
2" x 10" CAP

FILTER
FABRIC AS
SPEC.

NUT & WASHER

CORNER DTL.
SCALE: 1" = 1'-0"

14

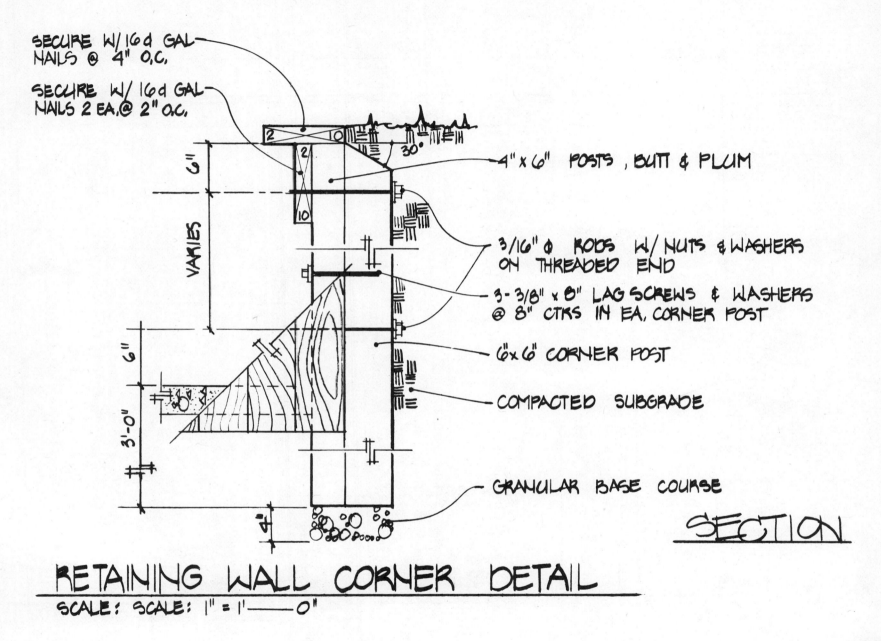

SECURE W/ 16d GAL NAILS @ 4" O.C.

SECURE W/ 16d GAL NAILS 2 EA.@ 2" O.C.

4"x 6" POSTS, BUTT & PLUM

3/16" φ RODS W/ NUTS & WASHERS ON THREADED END

3-3/8" x 8" LAG SCREWS & WASHERS @ 8" CTRS IN EA. CORNER POST

6"x 6" CORNER POST

COMPACTED SUBGRADE

GRANULAR BASE COURSE

SECTION

RETAINING WALL CORNER DETAIL
SCALE: SCALE: 1" = 1'——— O"

15

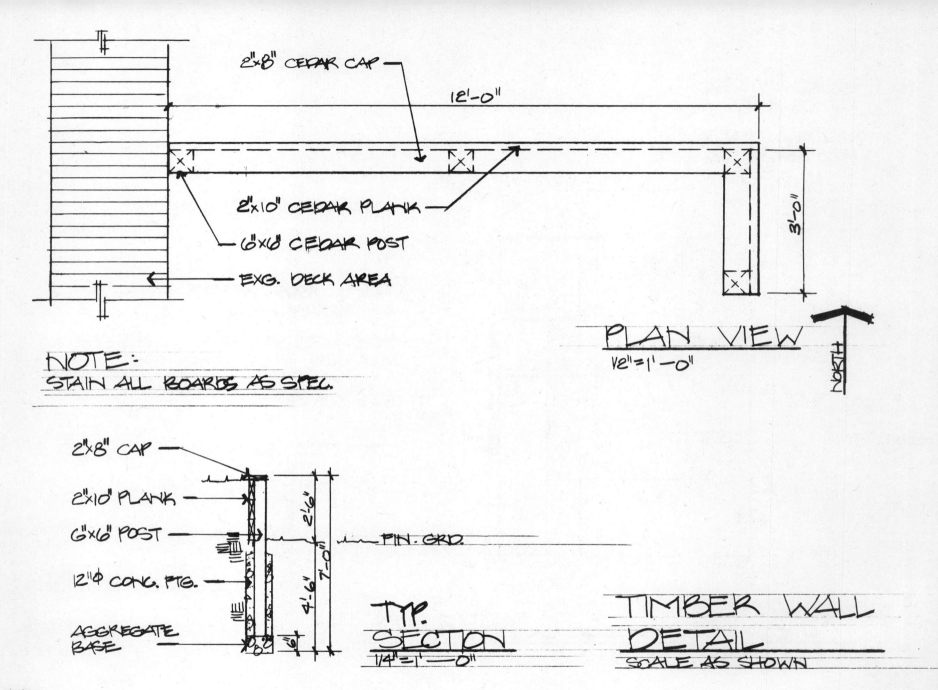

2"x8" CEDAR CAP

12'-0"

2"x10" CEDAR PLANK

6"x6" CEDAR POST

EXG. DECK AREA

3'-0"

PLAN VIEW
1/2"=1'-0"

NORTH

NOTE:
STAIN ALL BOARDS AS SPEC.

2"x8" CAP

2"x10" PLANK

6"x6" POST

12"ø CONC. FTG.

AGGREGATE BASE

2'-6"

7'-0"

4'-6"

6"

FIN. GRD.

TYP.
SECTION
1/4"=1'-0"

TIMBER WALL
DETAIL
SCALE AS SHOWN

16

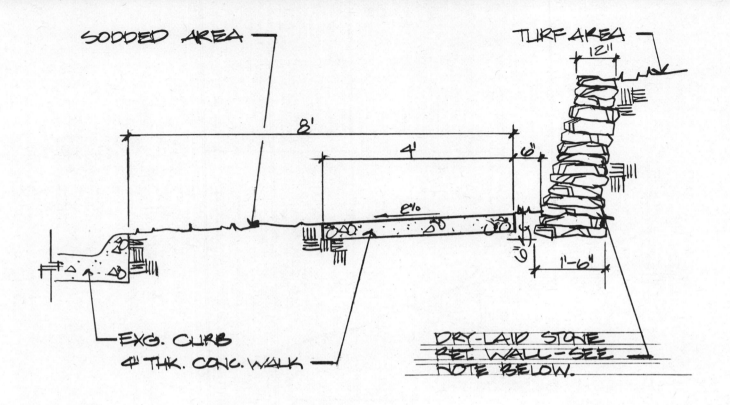

SODDED AREA

TURF AREA

12"

8'

4'

6"

6%

9"

1'-6"

EXG. CURB
4" THK. CONC. WALK

DRY-LAID STONE
RET. WALL - SEE
NOTE BELOW.

NOTE:
STONES TO BE NOMINALLY
• 3"-6" THK. QUARRY STONE - BASE
STONE TO BE 6"x12"x18"

• BATTER WALL 3" PER FOOT

• SPRIG WALL W/SEDUM STOLONIFERUM
2¼" POTS @ 24" O.C.

SECTION @
STONE WALL
NTS.

17

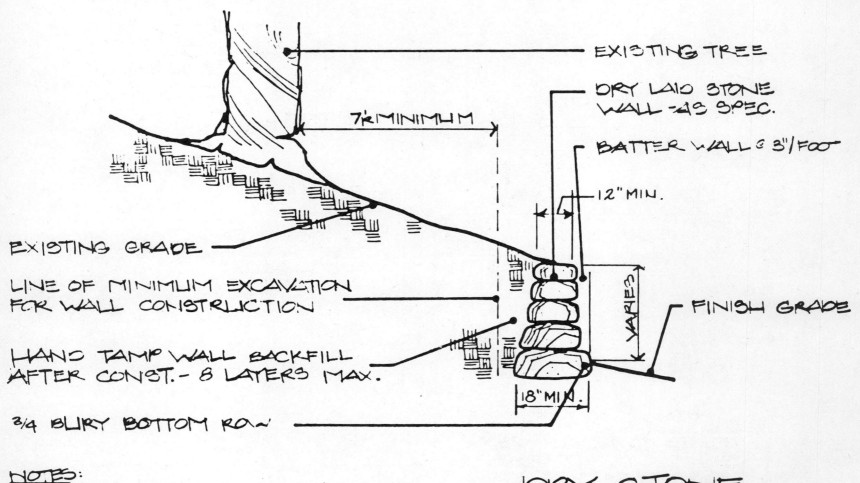

EXISTING TREE

DRY LAID STONE
WALL - AS SPEC.

BATTER WALL @ 3"/FOOT

12" MIN.

7½' MINIMUM

EXISTING GRADE

LINE OF MINIMUM EXCAVATION
FOR WALL CONSTRUCTION

HAND TAMP WALL BACKFILL
AFTER CONST. - 8 LAYERS MAX.

¾ BURY BOTTOM ROW

VARIES

FINISH GRADE

18" MIN.

NOTES:
TOP ROW OF STONES TO FOLLOW
EXISTING GRADE

STONES SHALL BE 6"x 12"x 18"
NOMINAL DIMENSION

DRY STONE
TREE WALL
NO SCALE

18

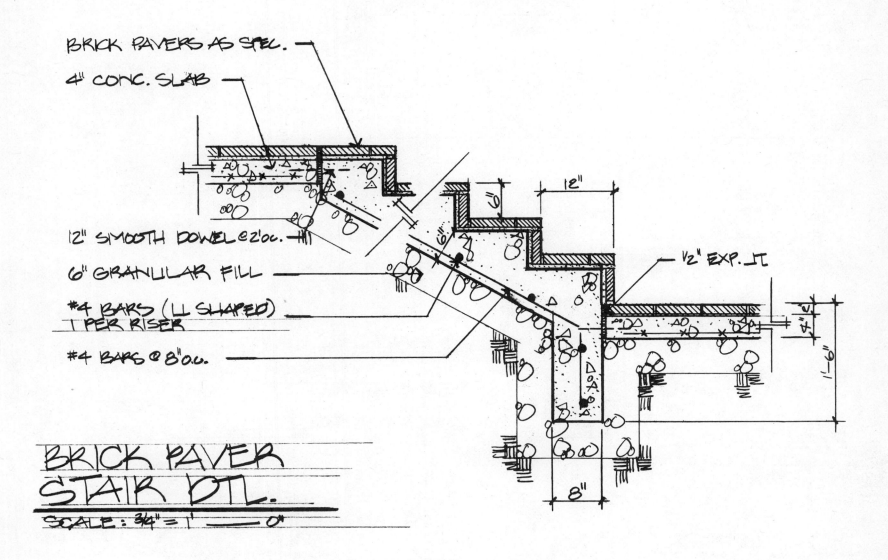

BRICK PAVERS AS SPEC.

4" CONC. SLAB

12" SMOOTH DOWEL @ 2' O.C.

6" GRANULAR FILL

#4 BARS (L SHAPED)
1 PER RISER

#4 BARS @ 8" O.C.

12"

6"

6"

½" EXP. JT.

5"

1'-6"

8"

BRICK PAVER
STAIR DTL.

SCALE: ¾" = 1' — 0"

19

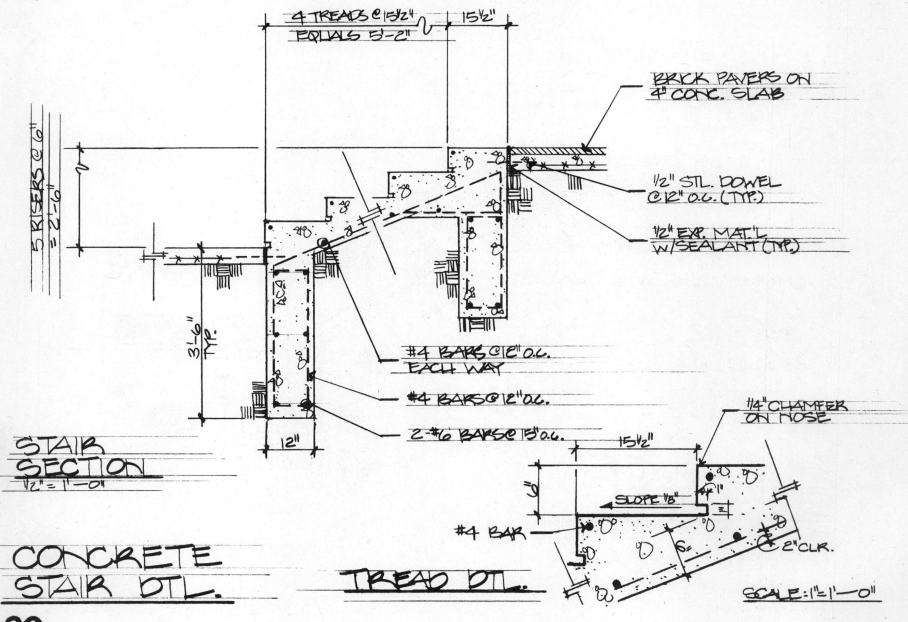

4 TREADS @ 15½" EQUALS 5'-2"

15½"

BRICK PAVERS ON 4" CONC. SLAB

5 RISERS @ 6" = 2'-6"

½" STL. DOWEL @ 12" O.C. (TYP.)

½" EXP. MAT'L W/ SEALANT (TYP.)

3'-6" TYP.

#4 BARS @ 12" O.C. EACH WAY

#4 BARS @ 12" O.C.

2-#6 BARS @ 13" O.C.

12"

STAIR SECTION
½" = 1'-0"

CONCRETE STAIR DTL.

20

TREAD DTL.

15½"

¾" CHAMFER ON NOSE

SLOPE ⅛"

#4 BAR

2" CLR.

SCALE: 1" = 1'-0"

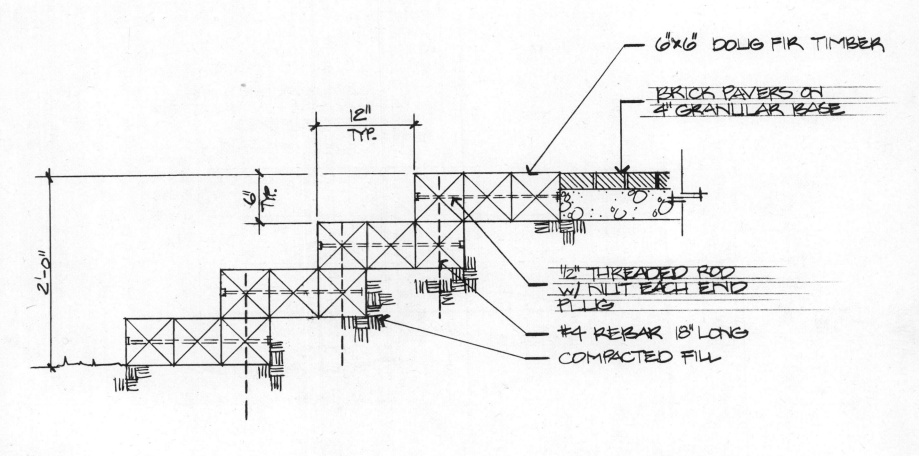

6"×6" DOUG FIR TIMBER

BRICK PAVERS ON
4" GRANULAR BASE

12"
TYP.

6" TYP.

2'-0"

1/2" THREADED ROD
W/ NUT EACH END
PLUG

#4 REBAR 18" LONG

COMPACTED FILL

SCALE: 1"=1'—0"

RAILROAD
TIE STEPS

21

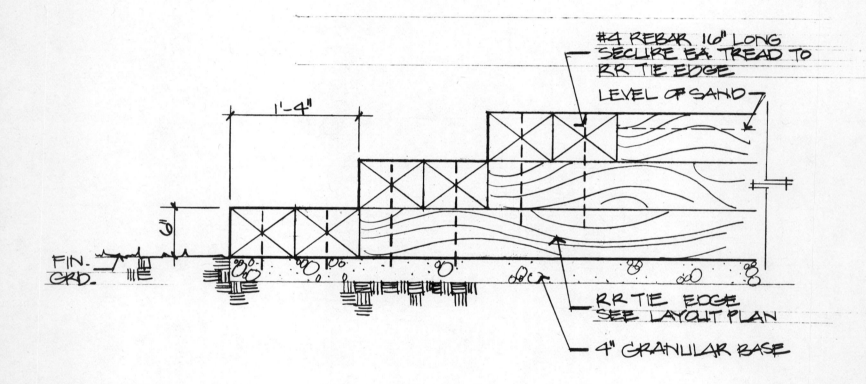

#4 REBAR 16" LONG
SECURE EA TREAD TO
RR TIE EDGE

LEVEL OF SAND

1'-4"

6"

FIN.
GRD.

RR TIE EDGE
SEE LAYOUT PLAN

4" GRANULAR BASE

RAILROAD TIE
EDGE / STEPS
SCALE: 1"=1'-0"

22

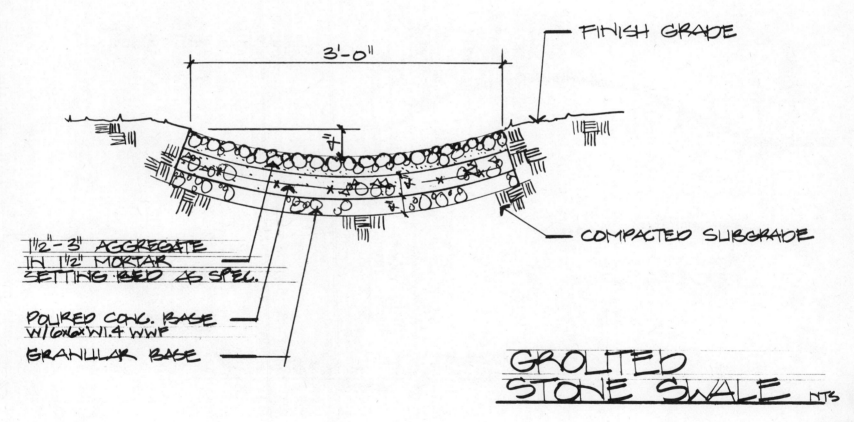

3'-0"

FINISH GRADE

COMPACTED SUBGRADE

1½"-3" AGGREGATE
IN 1½" MORTAR
SETTING BED AS SPEC.

POURED CONC. BASE
W/ 6x6xW1.4 WWF

GRANULAR BASE

GROUTED
STONE SWALE NTS

23

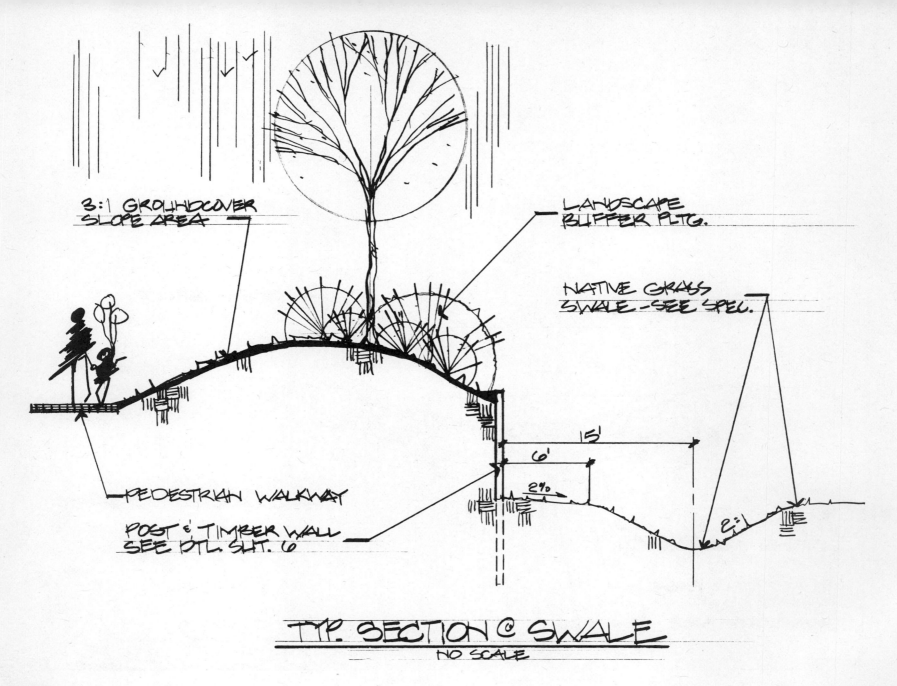

3:1 GROUNDCOVER
SLOPE AREA

LANDSCAPE
BUFFER PLTG.

NATIVE GRASS
SWALE - SEE SPEC.

15'

6'

2%

2:1

PEDESTRIAN WALKWAY

POST & TIMBER WALL
SEE DTL. SHT. 6

TYP. SECTION @ SWALE
NO SCALE

24

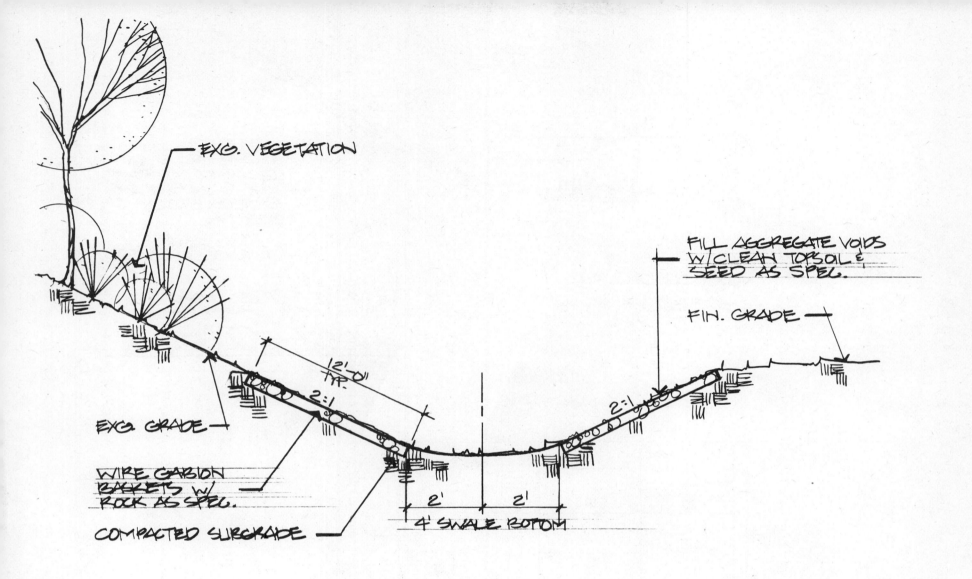

EXG. VEGETATION

FILL AGGREGATE VOIDS
W/ CLEAN TOPSOIL &
SEED AS SPEC.

FIN. GRADE

12'-0" TYP.

2:1

2:1

EXG. GRADE

WIRE GABION
BASKETS W/
ROCK AS SPEC.

COMPACTED SUBGRADE

2'   2'
4' SWALE BOTTOM

SECTION NOT TO SCALE

BANK
STABILIZATION DTL.

25

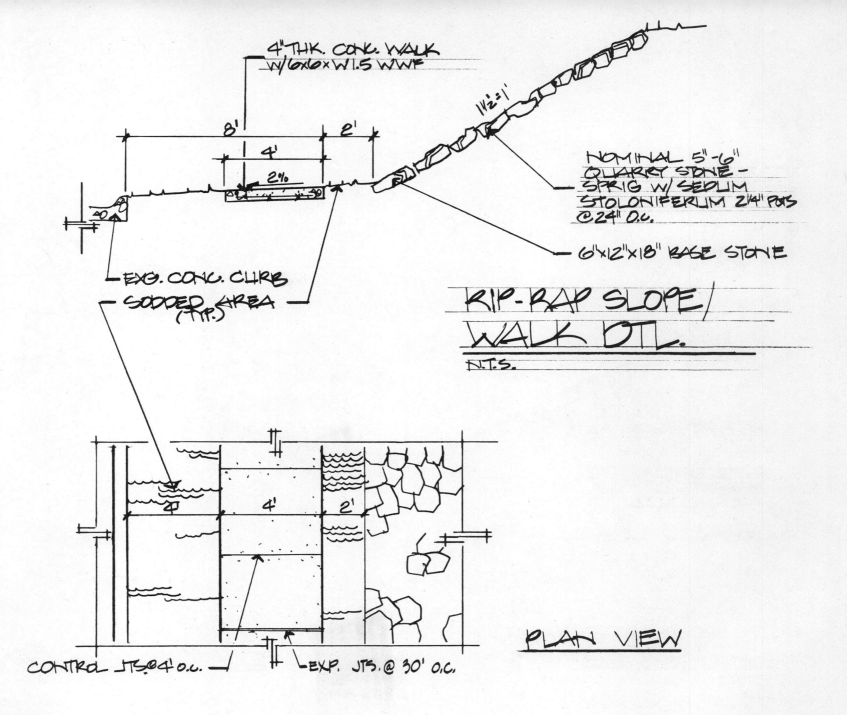

4" THK. CONC. WALK
W/ 6x6xW1.5 WWF

8'

2'

4'

2%

1½"=1'

NOMINAL 5"-6"
QUARRY STONE -
SPRIG W/ SEDUM
STOLONIFERUM 2¼" POTS
@ 24" O.C.

6"X12"X18" BASE STONE

EXG. CONC. CURB

SODDED AREA
(TYP.)

RIP-RAP SLOPE/
WALK DTL.

N.T.S.

4'

2'

CONTROL JTS. @ 4' O.C.

EXP. JTS. @ 30' O.C.

PLAN VIEW

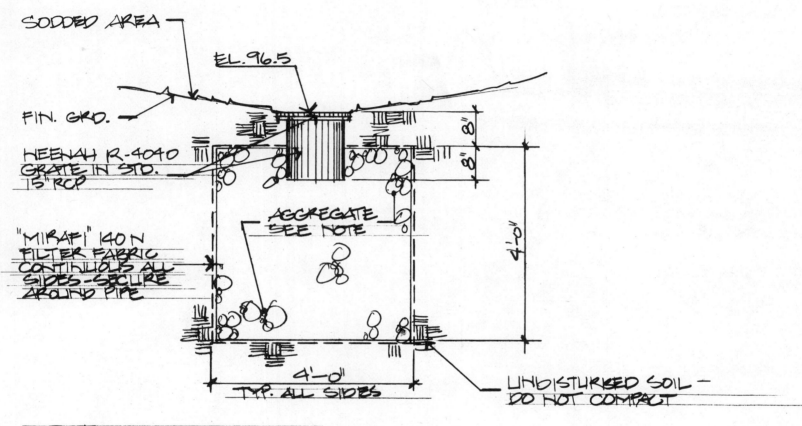

SODDED AREA

EL. 96.5

FIN. GRO.

HEENAH R-4040
GRATE IN STD.
15" RCP

"MIRAFI" 140 N
FILTER FABRIC
CONTINUOUS ALL
SIDES - SECURE
AROUND PIPE

8"

8"

4'-0"

AGGREGATE
SEE NOTE

4'-0"
TYP. ALL SIDES

UNDISTURBED SOIL -
DO NOT COMPACT

NOTE:
AGGREGATE TO BE STD. STATE
OF NEBRASKA FOUNDATION COURSE-
SUBMIT SAMPLE TO L.A. PRIOR
TO INSTALLATION

DRY-WELL
DETAIL ½"=1'-0"

27

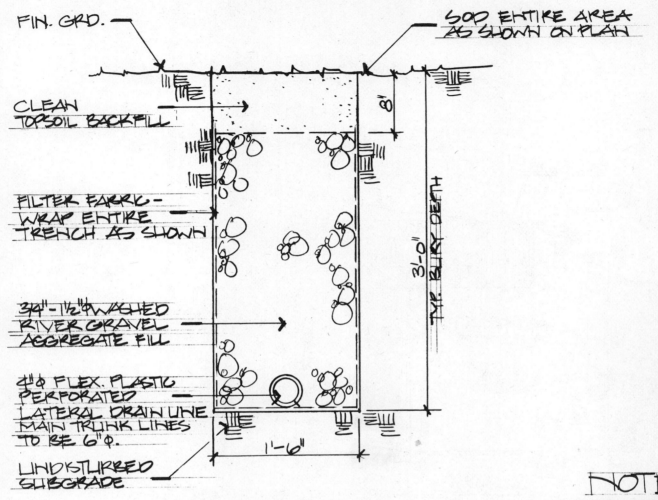

FIN. GRD.

SOD ENTIRE AREA
AS SHOWN ON PLAN

CLEAN
TOPSOIL BACKFILL

8"

3'-0" TYP. BURY DEPTH

FILTER FABRIC -
WRAP ENTIRE
TRENCH AS SHOWN

3/4"-1½"Ø WASHED
RIVER GRAVEL
AGGREGATE FILL

4"Ø FLEX. PLASTIC
PERFORATED
LATERAL DRAIN LINE
MAIN TRUNK LINES
TO BE 6"Ø.

UNDISTURBED
SUBGRADE

1'-6"

NOTE:
ALL LINE SPACING
TO BE 25' O.C. UNLESS
OTHERWISE SHOWN

DRAIN LINE DTL.
SCALE: 1"=1'-0"

28

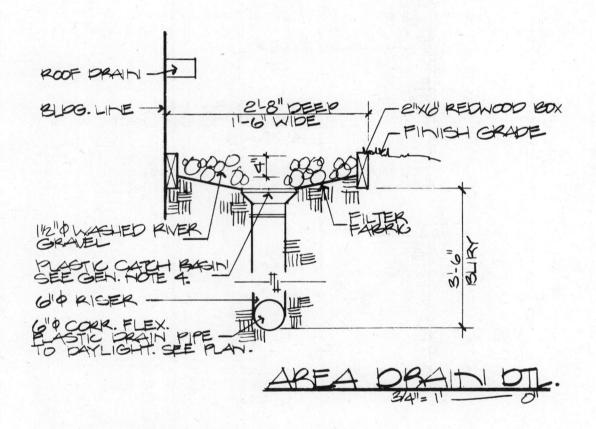

ROOF DRAIN →

BLDG. LINE →

2'-8" DEEP
1'-6" WIDE

2"X6" REDWOOD BOX

FINISH GRADE

4"

1½"Ø WASHED RIVER GRAVEL

FILTER FABRIC

PLASTIC CATCH BASIN SEE GEN. NOTE 4.

6"Ø RISER

6"Ø CORR. FLEX. PLASTIC DRAIN PIPE TO DAYLIGHT. SEE PLAN.

3'-6" BURY

AREA DRAIN DTL.
3/4" = 1'- 0"

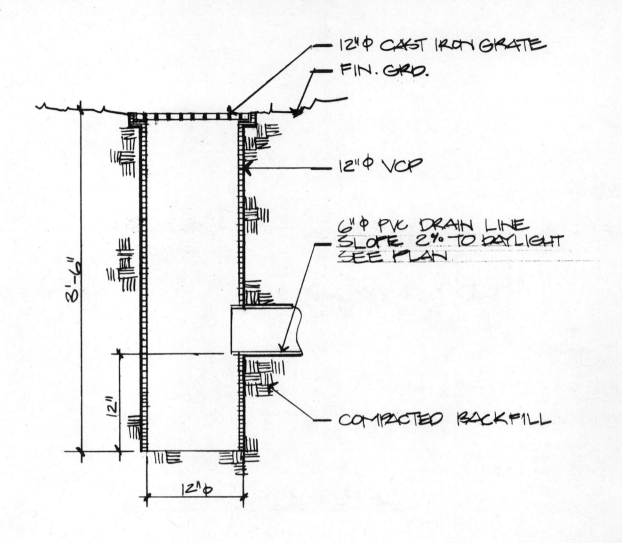

12"∅ CAST IRON GRATE

FIN. GRD.

12"∅ VCP

6"∅ PVC DRAIN LINE
SLOPE 2% TO DAYLIGHT
SEE PLAN

COMPACTED BACKFILL

8'-6"

12"

12"∅

LAWN DRAIN DTL.
SCALE: 1"=1'—0"

30

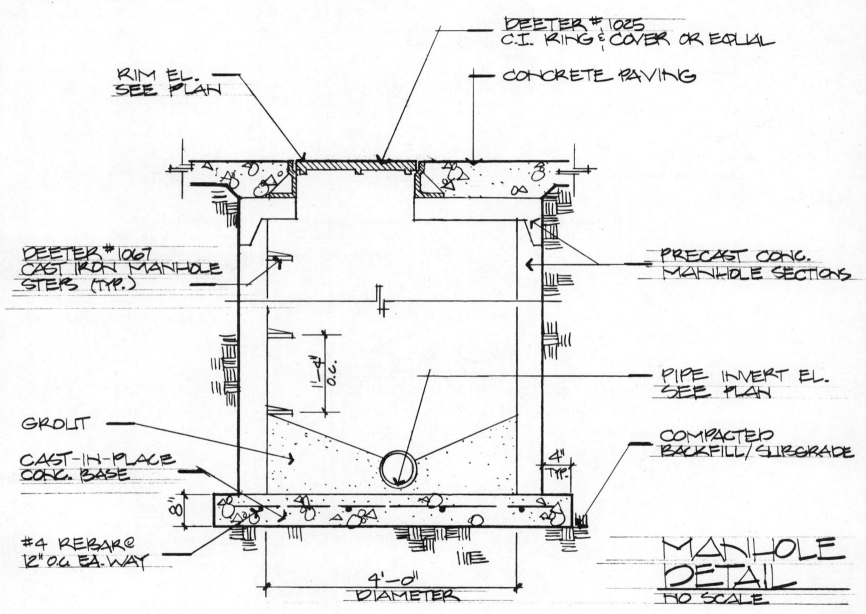

DEETER #1025
C.I. RING & COVER OR EQUAL

CONCRETE PAVING

RIM EL.
SEE PLAN

DEETER #1067
CAST IRON MANHOLE
STEPS (TYP.)

PRECAST CONC.
MANHOLE SECTIONS

1'-4"
O.C.

PIPE INVERT EL.
SEE PLAN

GROUT

COMPACTED
BACKFILL/SUBGRADE

CAST-IN-PLACE
CONC. BASE

4"
TYP.

8"

#4 REBAR@
12" O.C. EA. WAY

4'-0"
DIAMETER

MANHOLE
DETAIL
NO SCALE

31

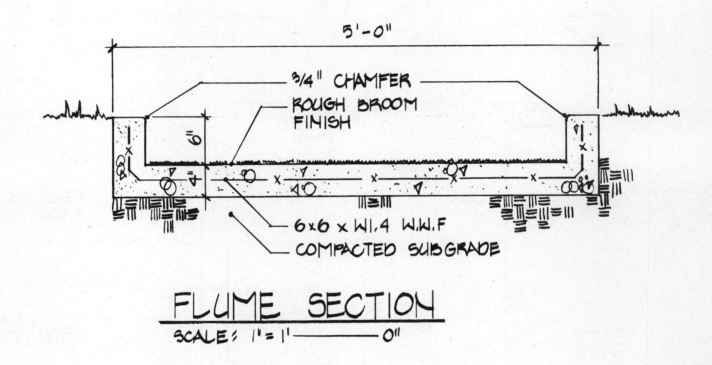

5'-0"

3/4" CHAMFER

ROUGH BROOM
FINISH

6"

4"

6x6 x W1.4 W.W.F

COMPACTED SUBGRADE

FLUME SECTION
SCALE: 1" = 1' ————— 0"

32

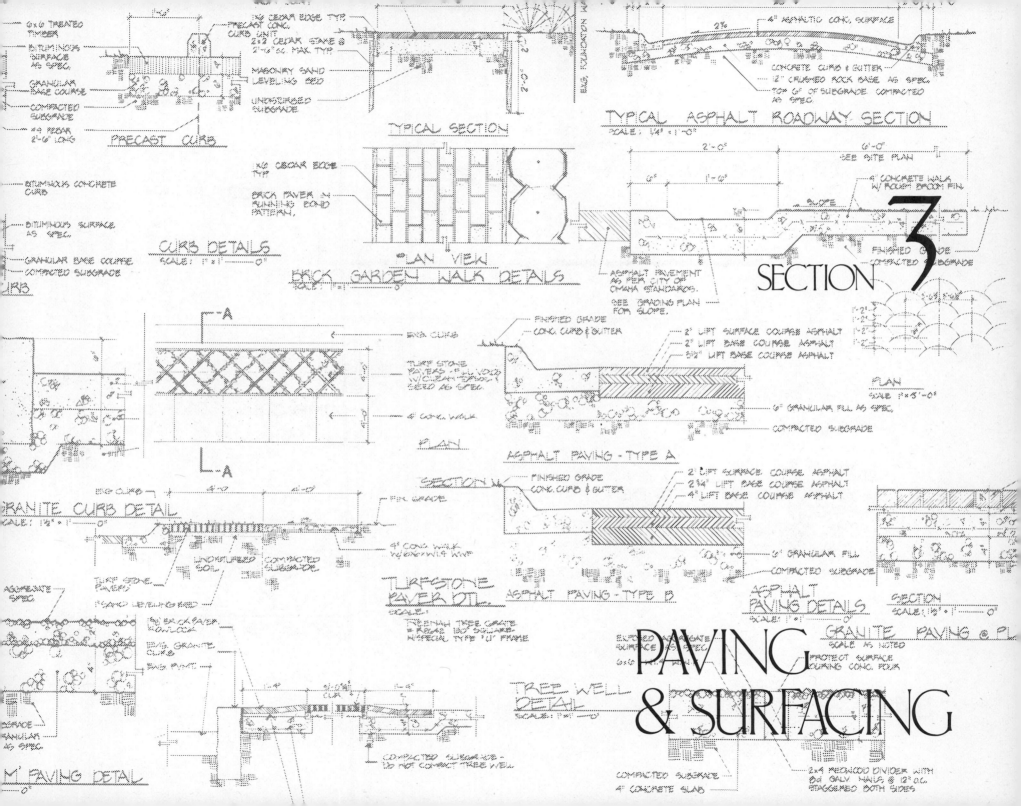

PAVING & SURFACING

SECTION 3

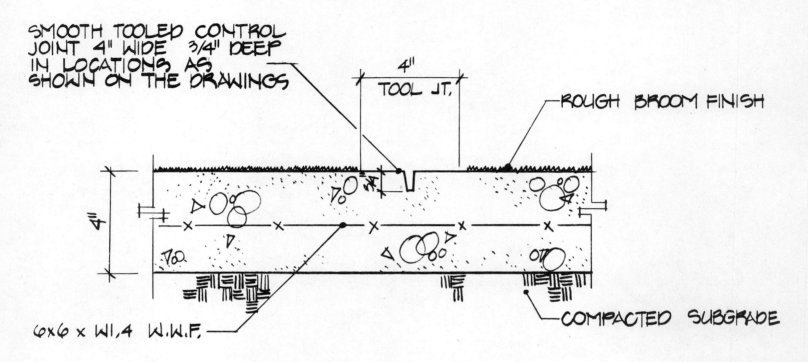

SMOOTH TOOLED CONTROL
JOINT 4" WIDE 3/4" DEEP
IN LOCATIONS AS
SHOWN ON THE DRAWINGS

4"
TOOL JT.

ROUGH BROOM FINISH

4"

COMPACTED SUBGRADE

6x6 x W1,4 W.W.F.

NOTE:
1/2" EXPANSION JT. TO BE
SPACED AS SHOWN ON
THE DRAWINGS OR
MAX. 30' O.C.

4" CONCRETE
WALK DETAIL
SCALE: 3"=1'——0"

34

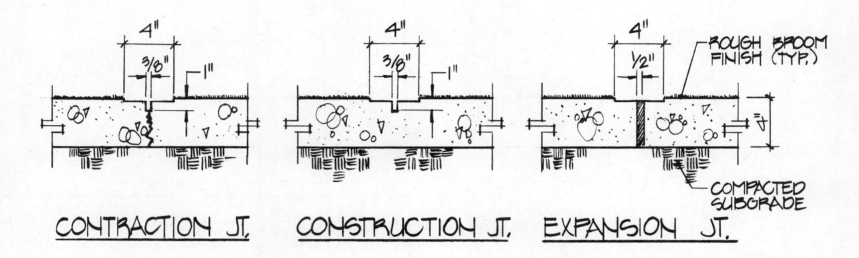

CONTRACTION JT.   CONSTRUCTION JT.   EXPANSION JT.

NOTES:
1. SPACING OF ALL JOINTS TO BE AS SHOWN
   ON PLANS AND/OR SPECS.
2. EXPANSION JOINTS TO BE 30' O.C. MAX.

CONCRETE WALK JOINT DETAILS
SCALE: 1½" = 1'————— 0"

35

OVER 4" CONC. SUB SLAB (4000 PSI)
REINFORCED W/ 6x6x10/1.0 WWF

*NOTE: 4" SUB-SLAB TO BE ALLOW-
ED 28 DAYS TO CURE BEFORE
INSTALLING 2" BOMANITE

HAND TOOLED CONTROL JOINT

4000 PSI CONC. 6" THICK W/ HEAVY
BROOM FINISH

EXISTING OR NEW 8'x8' CONC. PANELS W/
1"x3" REDWOOD DIVIDERS - WHERE
NEW CONC. MEETS NEW CONC. USE
1/2" PREMOLDED EXPANSION
MATERIAL OR 1x3½ AS PER PLAN

COMPACTED SAND SUBGRADE 6" MIN.

NEW BOMANITE @ EXISTING CONC. SURFACING

SCALE: 1½" = 1'-0"

36

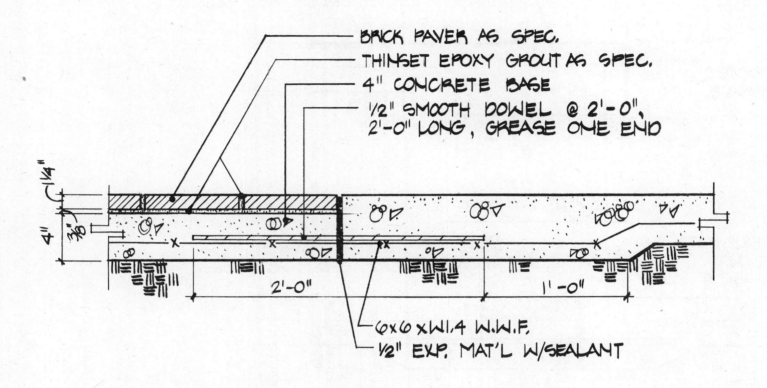

BRICK PAVER AS SPEC.

THINSET EPOXY GROUT AS SPEC.

4" CONCRETE BASE

1/2" SMOOTH DOWEL @ 2'-0",
2'-0" LONG, GREASE ONE END

1 1/4"

3/8"

4"

2'-0"

1'-0"

6x6 x W1.4 W.W.F.

1/2" EXP. MAT'L W/SEALANT

BRICK PAVING
SCALE: 1 1/2" = 1'——0"

37

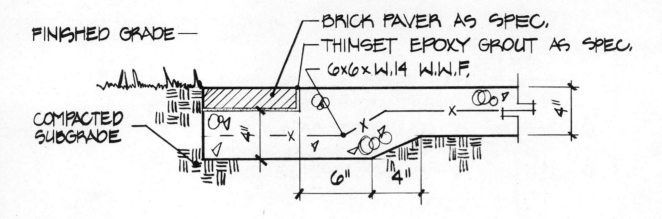

FINISHED GRADE —

BRICK PAVER AS SPEC.
THINSET EPOXY GROUT AS SPEC.
6×6×W.14 W.W.F.

COMPACTED SUBGRADE

4"

6"   4"

BRICK EDGE

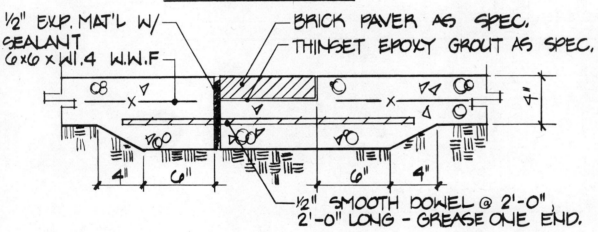

½" EXP. MAT'L W/ SEALANT
6×6×WI.4 W.W.F

BRICK PAVER AS SPEC.
THINSET EPOXY GROUT AS SPEC.

4"

4"   6"   6"   4"

½" SMOOTH DOWEL @ 2'-0",
2'-0" LONG - GREASE ONE END.

BRICK INLAY

BRICK/PAVEMENT DETAILS
SCALE: 1½" = 1'   0"

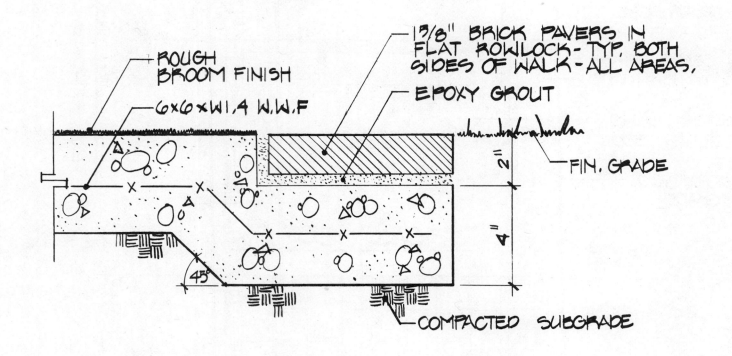

ROUGH
BROOM FINISH

6×6×W1.4 W.W.F

1⅜" BRICK PAVERS IN
FLAT ROWLOCK - TYP. BOTH
SIDES OF WALK - ALL AREAS.

EPOXY GROUT

FIN. GRADE

2"

4"

45°

COMPACTED SUBGRADE

BRICK EDGING DETAIL
SCALE: 3" = 1' — 0"

39

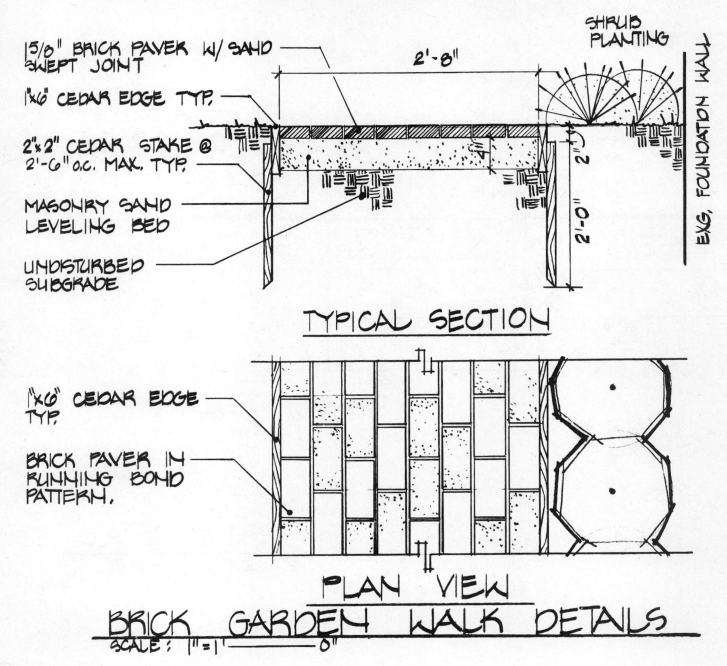

15/8" BRICK PAVER W/ SAND SWEPT JOINT

1"x6" CEDAR EDGE TYP.

2"x2" CEDAR STAKE @ 2'-6" O.C. MAX. TYP.

MASONRY SAND LEVELING BED

UNDISTURBED SUBGRADE

SHRUB PLANTING

EXG. FOUNDATION WALL

2'-8"

4"

2"

2'-0"

TYPICAL SECTION

1"x6" CEDAR EDGE TYP.

BRICK PAVER IN RUNNING BOND PATTERN.

PLAN VIEW

BRICK GARDEN WALK DETAILS

SCALE: 1"=1'-0"

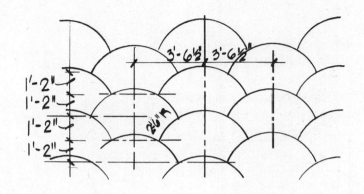

3'-6½" | 3'-6½"

1'-2"
1'-2"
1'-2"
1'-2"

2'-0"

PLAN

SCALE 1"=5'-0"

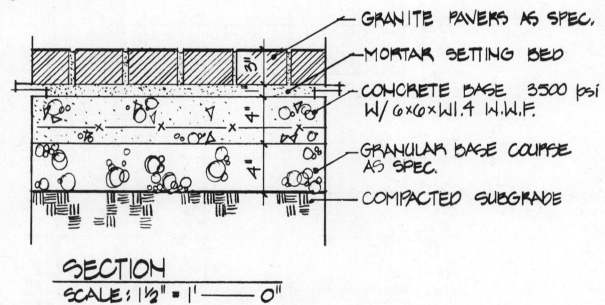

GRANITE PAVERS AS SPEC.

MORTAR SETTING BED

CONCRETE BASE 3500 psi
W/ 6×6×W1.4 W.W.F.

GRANULAR BASE COURSE
AS SPEC.

COMPACTED SUBGRADE

3"

4"

4"

SECTION

SCALE: 1½" = 1'————0"

GRANITE PAVING @ PLAZA

SCALE AS NOTED

41

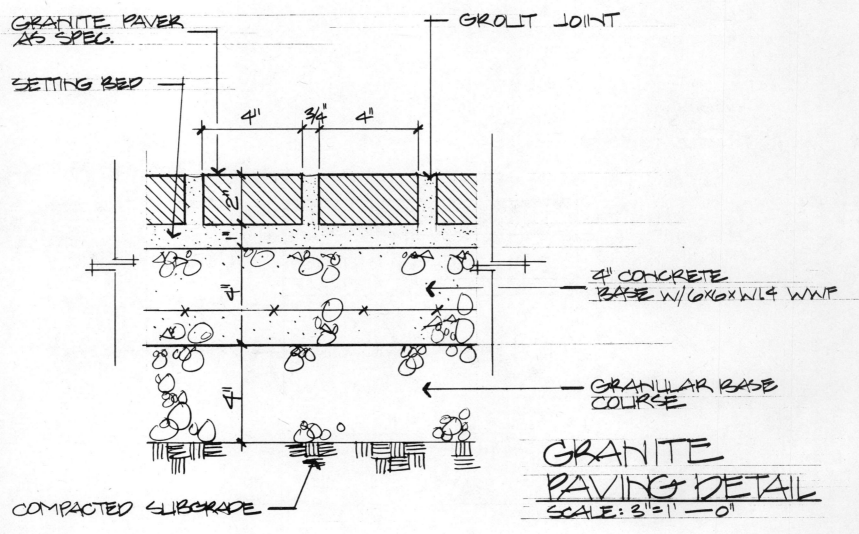

GRANITE PAVER
AS SPEC.

GROUT JOINT

SETTING BED

4"   3/4"   4"

2"

4" CONCRETE
BASE W/6x6xWL4 WWF

GRANULAR BASE
COURSE

COMPACTED SUBGRADE

GRANITE
PAVING DETAIL
SCALE: 3"=1'—0"

42

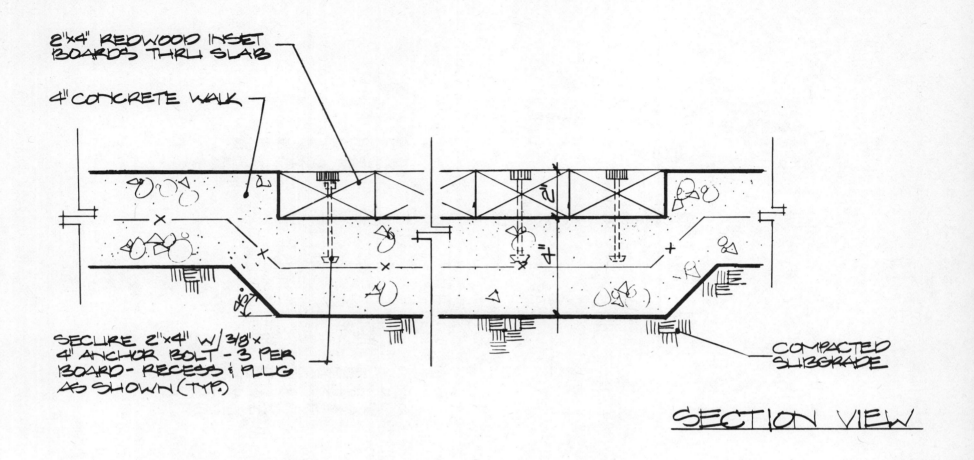

2"x4" REDWOOD INSET
BOARDS THRU SLAB

4" CONCRETE WALK

SECURE 2"x4" W/ 3/8" x
4" ANCHOR BOLT - 3 PER
BOARD - RECESS & PLUG
AS SHOWN (TYP.)

COMPACTED
SUBGRADE

SECTION VIEW

(6/5) WOOD INSET

SCALE: 3" = 1'-0"

43

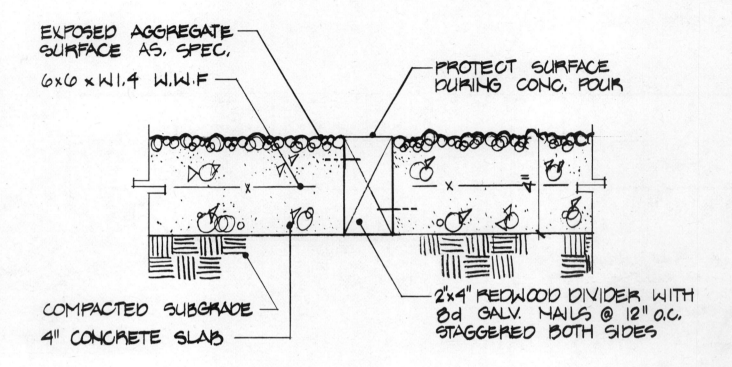

EXPOSED AGGREGATE
SURFACE AS. SPEC.

6×6 × W1.4 W.W.F

PROTECT SURFACE
DURING CONC. POUR

COMPACTED SUBGRADE

4" CONCRETE SLAB

2"×4" REDWOOD DIVIDER WITH
8d GALV. NAILS @ 12" O.C.
STAGGERED BOTH SIDES

REDWOOD DIVIDER STRIP
SCALE: 3" = 1'————————— 0"

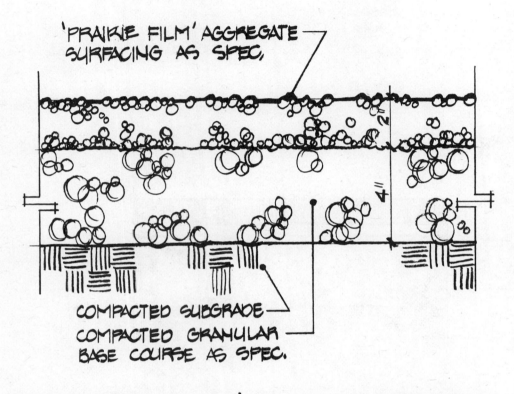

'PRAIRIE FILM' AGGREGATE
SURFACING AS SPEC.

2"

4"

COMPACTED SUBGRADE
COMPACTED GRANULAR
BASE COURSE AS SPEC.

'PRAIRIE FILM' PAVING DETAIL
SCALE: 3" = 1'————0"

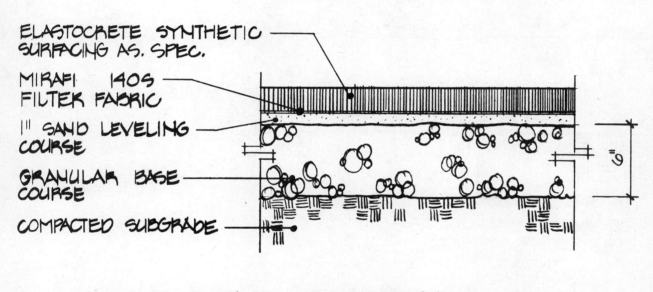

ELASTOCRETE SYNTHETIC
SURFACING AS. SPEC.

MIRAFI 140S
FILTER FABRIC

1" SAND LEVELING
COURSE

GRANULAR BASE
COURSE

COMPACTED SUBGRADE

6"

SYNTHETIC SURFACING DTL.

SCALE: 1" = 1'————————0"

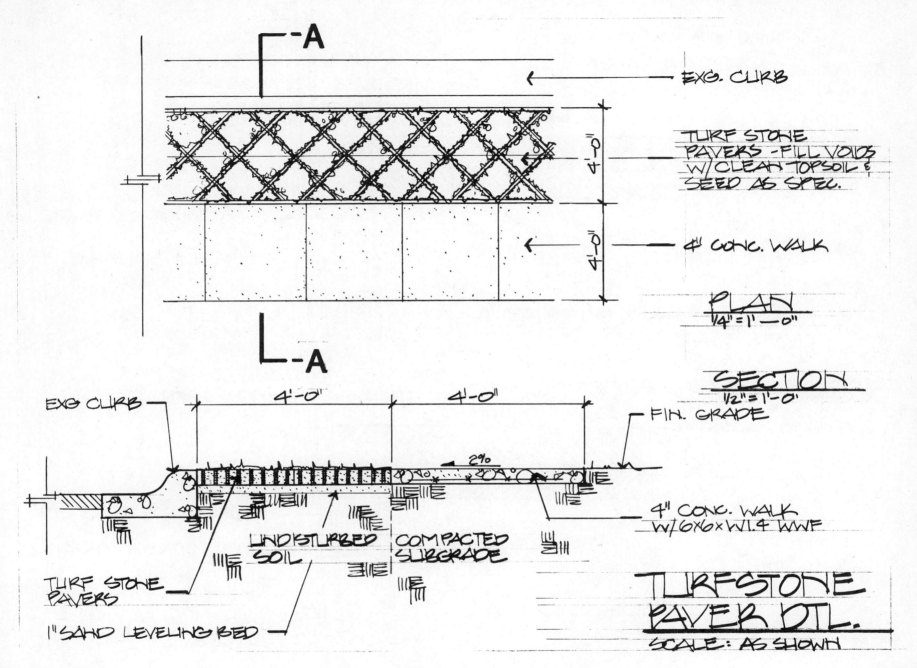

-A

L-A

EXG. CURB

TURF STONE PAVERS -FILL VOIDS W/ CLEAN TOPSOIL & SEED AS SPEC.

4'-0"

4'-0"

4" CONC. WALK

PLAN
1/4" = 1'-0"

SECTION
1/2" = 1'-0"

EXG CURB

4'-0"

4'-0"

FIN. GRADE

2%

4" CONC. WALK
W/ 6x6 x W1.4 WWF

UNDISTURBED SOIL

COMPACTED SUBGRADE

TURF STONE PAVERS

1" SAND LEVELING BED

TURFSTONE
PAVER DTL.
SCALE: AS SHOWN

47

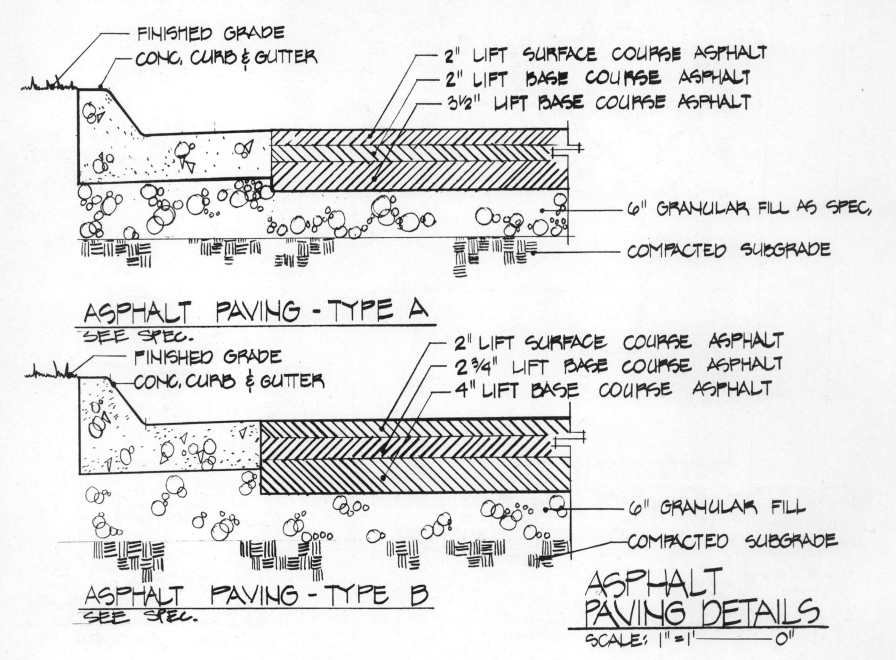

FINISHED GRADE
CONC. CURB & GUTTER

2" LIFT SURFACE COURSE ASPHALT
2" LIFT BASE COURSE ASPHALT
3½" LIFT BASE COURSE ASPHALT

6" GRANULAR FILL AS SPEC.

COMPACTED SUBGRADE

ASPHALT PAVING - TYPE A
SEE SPEC.

FINISHED GRADE
CONC. CURB & GUTTER

2" LIFT SURFACE COURSE ASPHALT
2¾" LIFT BASE COURSE ASPHALT
4" LIFT BASE COURSE ASPHALT

6" GRANULAR FILL

COMPACTED SUBGRADE

ASPHALT PAVING - TYPE B
SEE SPEC.

ASPHALT
PAVING DETAILS
SCALE: 1" = 1'————0"

48

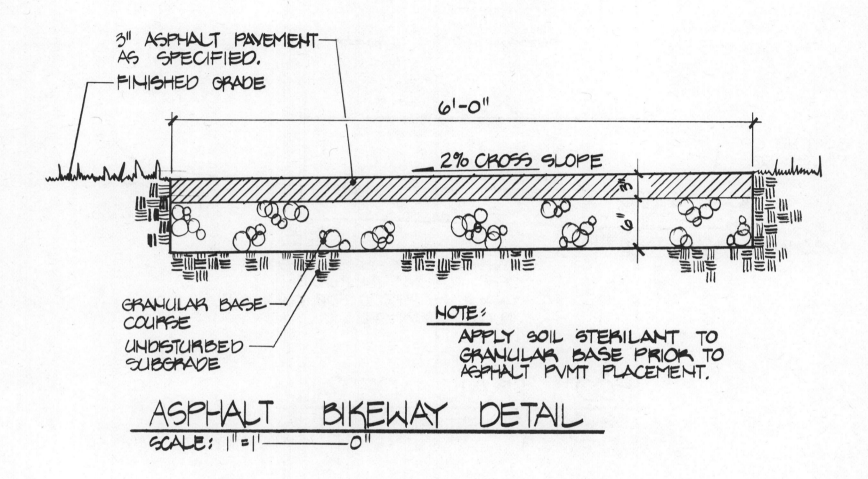

3" ASPHALT PAVEMENT
AS SPECIFIED.

FINISHED GRADE

6'-0"

2% CROSS SLOPE

3"

6"

GRANULAR BASE
COURSE

UNDISTURBED
SUBGRADE

NOTE:
APPLY SOIL STERILANT TO
GRANULAR BASE PRIOR TO
ASPHALT PVMT PLACEMENT.

ASPHALT BIKEWAY DETAIL
SCALE: 1"=1'————0"

49

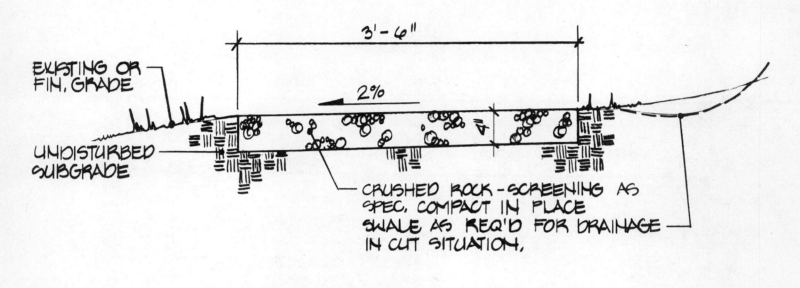

EXISTING OR
FIN. GRADE

3' - 6"

2%

UNDISTURBED
SUBGRADE

4"

CRUSHED ROCK - SCREENING AS
SPEC. COMPACT IN PLACE
SWALE AS REQ'D FOR DRAINAGE
IN CUT SITUATION,

FOOT TRAIL DETAIL
SCALE: 1" = 1' —— 0"

50

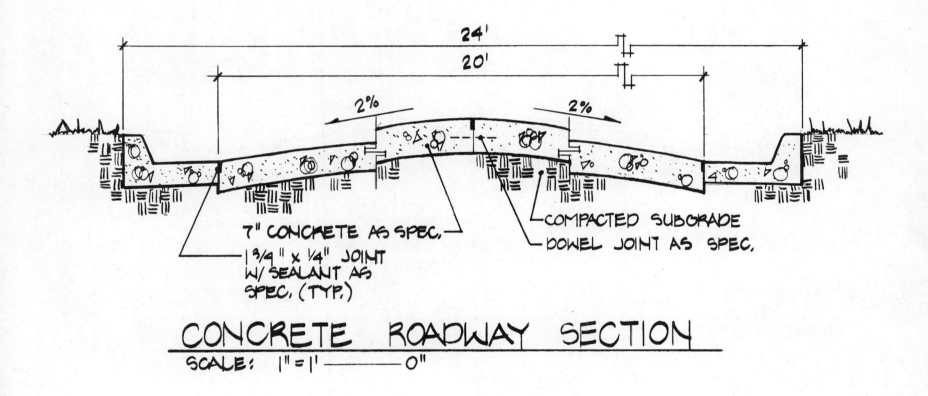

24'

20'

2%　　　　　　2%

7" CONCRETE AS SPEC.

1 3/4" x 1/4" JOINT
W/ SEALANT AS
SPEC. (TYP.)

COMPACTED SUBGRADE

DOWEL JOINT AS SPEC.

CONCRETE ROADWAY SECTION
SCALE:　1" = 1' ——— 0"

51

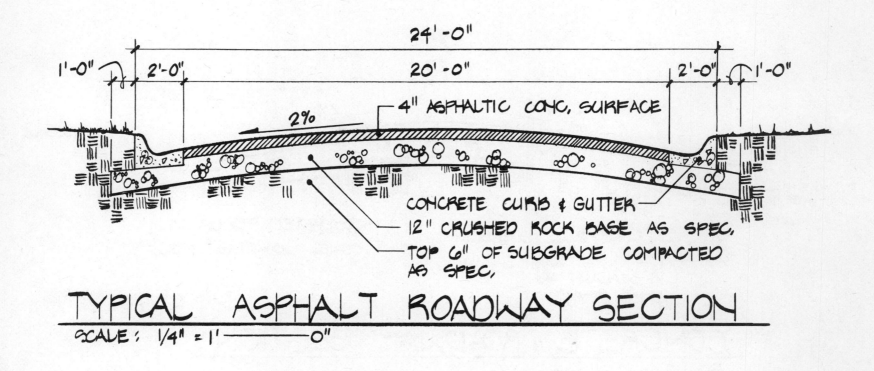

24'-0"

20'-0"

1'-0" 2'-0" 2'-0" 1'-0"

4" ASPHALTIC CONC. SURFACE

2%

CONCRETE CURB & GUTTER

12" CRUSHED ROCK BASE AS SPEC.

TOP 6" OF SUBGRADE COMPACTED AS SPEC.

TYPICAL ASPHALT ROADWAY SECTION

SCALE: 1/4" = 1'————0"

52

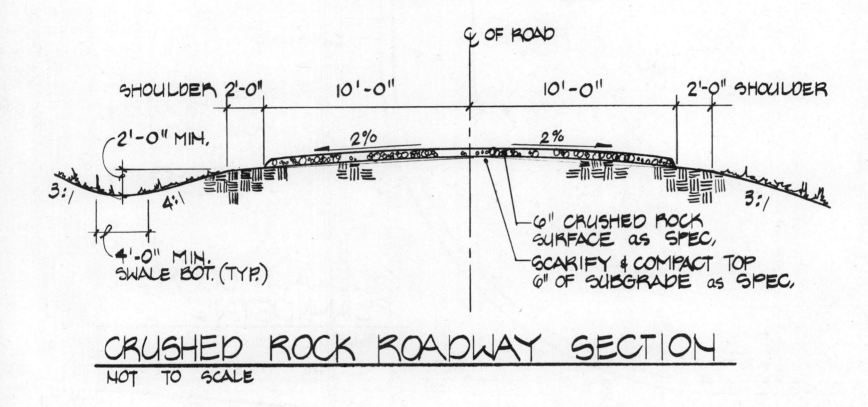

CRUSHED ROCK ROADWAY SECTION

NOT TO SCALE

53

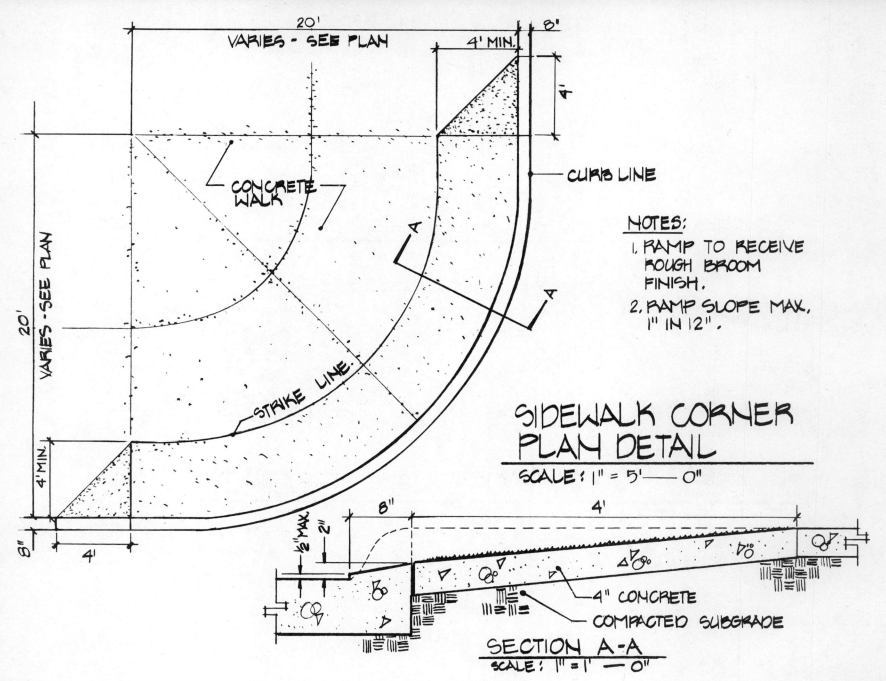

20'
VARIES - SEE PLAN

8'

4' MIN.

4'

CONCRETE WALK

CURB LINE

20'
VARIES - SEE PLAN

A

A

STRIKE LINE

NOTES:
1. RAMP TO RECEIVE ROUGH BROOM FINISH.
2. RAMP SLOPE MAX. 1" IN 12".

4' MIN.

8'

4'

SIDEWALK CORNER PLAN DETAIL
SCALE: 1" = 5' — 0"

8'

4'

½" MAX.

2"

4" CONCRETE

COMPACTED SUBGRADE

SECTION A-A
SCALE: 1" = 1' — 0"

54

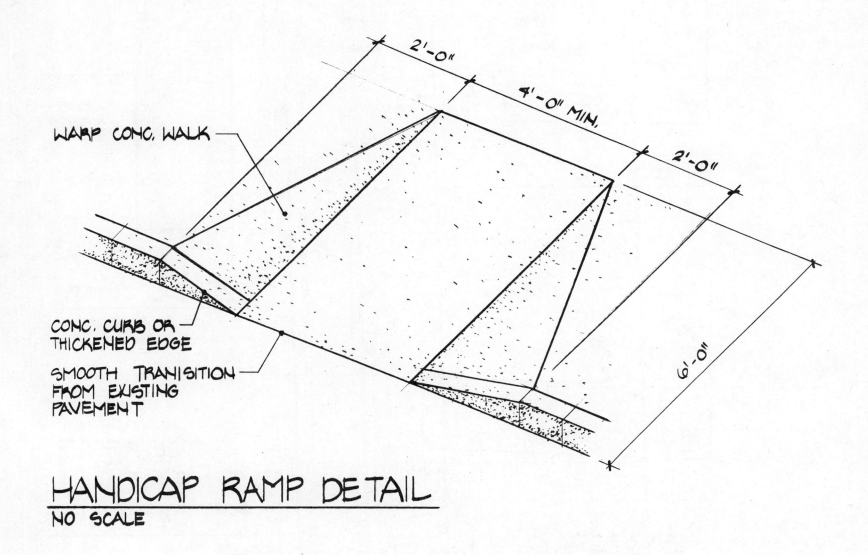

WARP CONC. WALK

2'-0"

4'-0" MIN.

2'-0"

CONC. CURB OR
THICKENED EDGE

SMOOTH TRANSITION
FROM EXISTING
PAVEMENT

6'-0"

HANDICAP RAMP DETAIL
NO SCALE

55

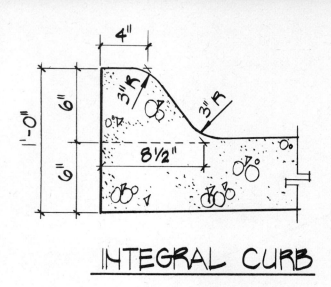

INTEGRAL CURB

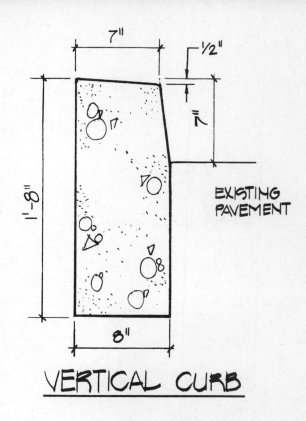

VERTICAL CURB

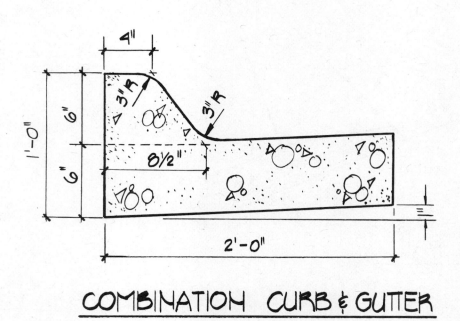

COMBINATION CURB & GUTTER

6" CONCRETE
PAVEMENT
CURB DETAILS

SCALE: 1½" = 1'——0"

56

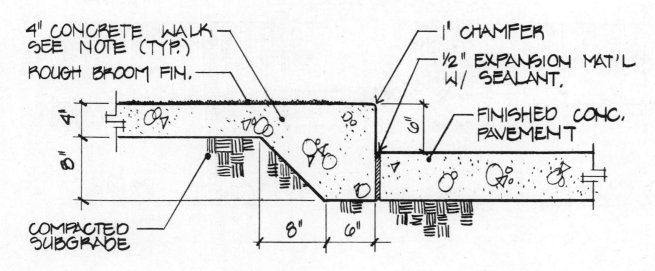

4" CONCRETE WALK
SEE NOTE (TYP.)

ROUGH BROOM FIN.

1" CHAMFER

½" EXPANSION MAT'L
W/ SEALANT.

FINISHED CONC.
PAVEMENT

COMPACTED
SUBGRADE

4"

8"

6"

8"

6"

NOTE:
EXPANSION JOINTS IN 4" CONCRETE
WALK SHALL BE PLACED @
30' O.C. MAX,

THICKENED
EDGE DETAIL
SCALE: 1"= 1'——0"

57

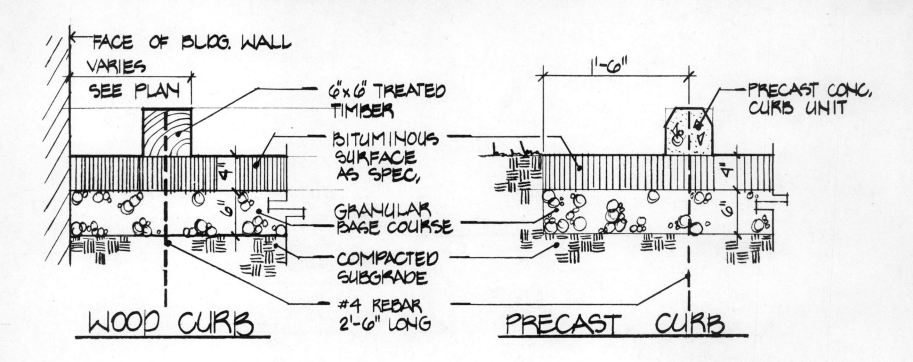

FACE OF BLDG. WALL
VARIES
SEE PLAN

6"x6" TREATED TIMBER

BITUMINOUS SURFACE AS SPEC.

GRANULAR BASE COURSE

COMPACTED SUBGRADE

#4 REBAR 2'-6" LONG

WOOD CURB

1'-6"

PRECAST CONC. CURB UNIT

PRECAST CURB

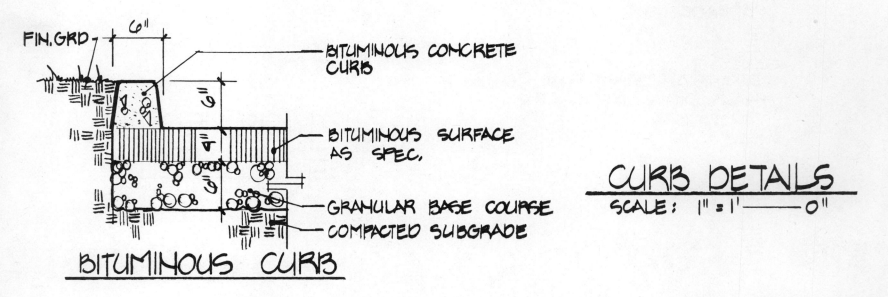

FIN.GRD

6"

BITUMINOUS CONCRETE CURB

BITUMINOUS SURFACE AS SPEC.

GRANULAR BASE COURSE
COMPACTED SUBGRADE

BITUMINOUS CURB

CURB DETAILS
SCALE: 1" = 1'————0"

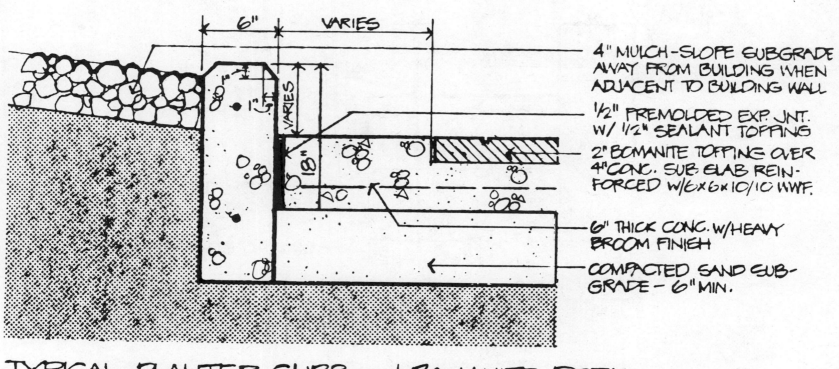

6"   VARIES

VARIES

18"

1"

1"

4" MULCH-SLOPE SUBGRADE
AWAY FROM BUILDING WHEN
ADJACENT TO BUILDING WALL

1/2" PREMOLDED EXP. JNT.
W/ 1/2" SEALANT TOPPING

2" BOMANITE TOPPING OVER
4" CONC. SUB-SLAB REIN-
FORCED W/ 6x6x10/10 WWF.

6" THICK CONC. W/HEAVY
BROOM FINISH

COMPACTED SAND SUB-
GRADE - 6" MIN.

TYPICAL PLANTER CURB and BOMANITE DETAIL

SCALE 1 1/2" = 1' 0"

59

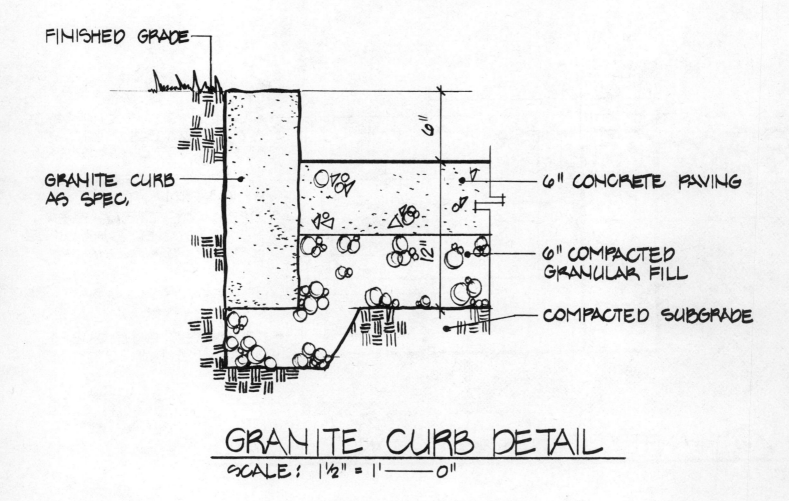

FINISHED GRADE

GRANITE CURB
AS SPEC.

6"

6" CONCRETE PAVING

12"

6" COMPACTED
GRANULAR FILL

COMPACTED SUBGRADE

GRANITE CURB DETAIL
SCALE: 1½" = 1'———0"

60

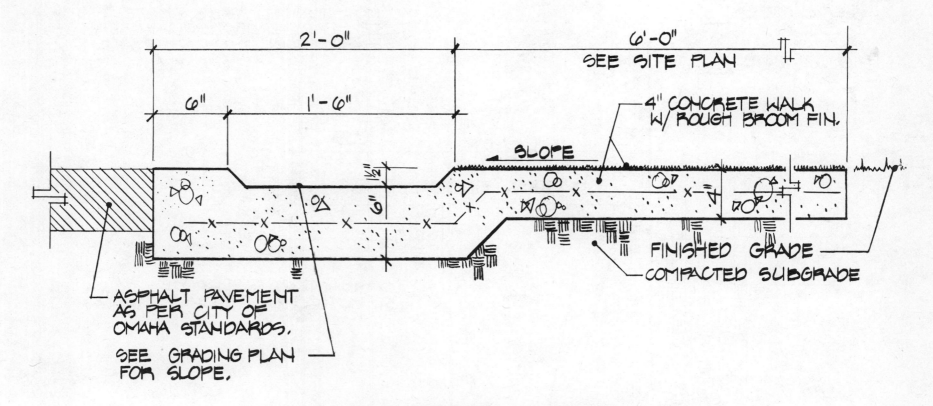

2'-0"

6'-0"
SEE SITE PLAN

6"

1'-6"

4" CONCRETE WALK
W/ ROUGH BROOM FIN.

SLOPE

½"

6"

ASPHALT PAVEMENT
AS PER CITY OF
OMAHA STANDARDS.

SEE GRADING PLAN
FOR SLOPE.

FINISHED GRADE

COMPACTED SUBGRADE

CONCRETE WHEEL DIP
SCALE: 1½" = 1' ———— 0"

61

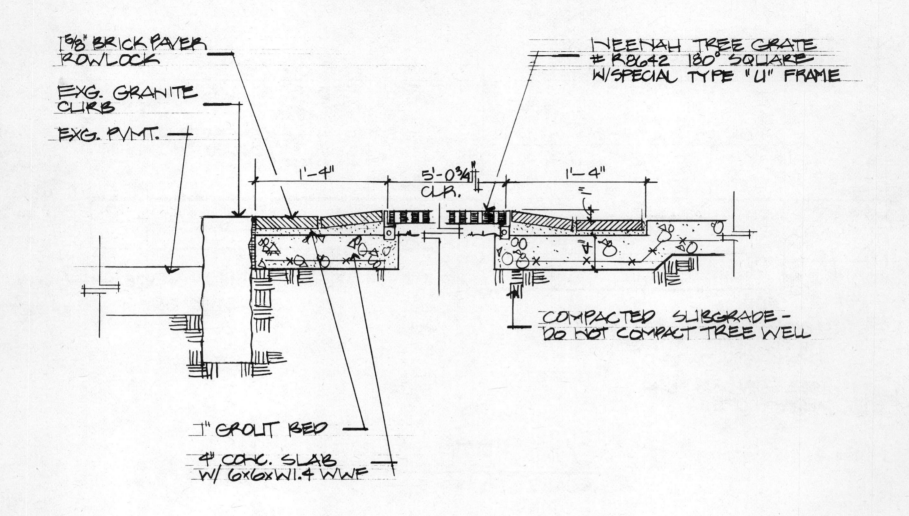

1⅝" BRICK PAVER ROWLOCK

EXG. GRANITE CURB

EXG. PVMT.

NEENAH TREE GRATE #R8642 180° SQUARE W/SPECIAL TYPE "U" FRAME

1'-4"

5'-0¾" CLR.

1'-4"

COMPACTED SUBGRADE - DO NOT COMPACT TREE WELL

1" GROUT BED

4" CONC. SLAB W/ 6x6xW1.4 WWF

TREE WELL DETAIL
SCALE: 1"=1'—0"

62

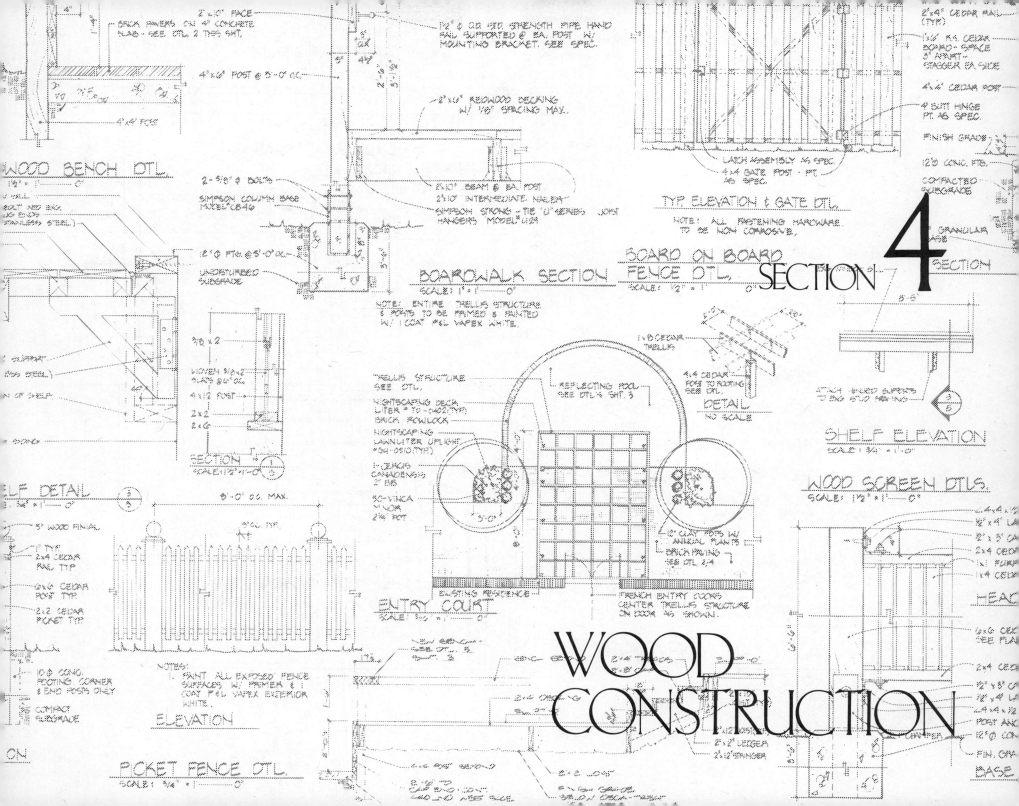

WOOD CONSTRUCTION

SECTION 4

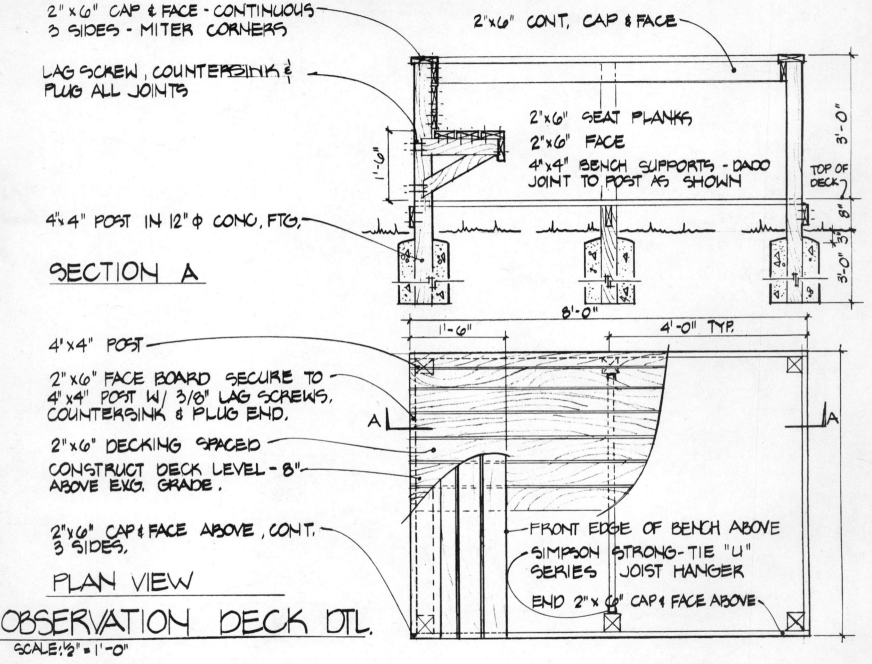

2" x 6" CAP & FACE - CONTINUOUS - 3 SIDES - MITER CORNERS

LAG SCREW, COUNTERSINK & PLUG ALL JOINTS

4" x 4" POST IN 12" ⌀ CONC. FTG.

SECTION A

2" x 6" CONT. CAP & FACE

2" x 6" SEAT PLANKS
2" x 6" FACE
4" x 4" BENCH SUPPORTS - DADO JOINT TO POST AS SHOWN

1'-6"

3'-0"

TOP OF DECK

8"

3"

3'-0"

8'-0"

1'-6"

4'-0" TYP.

4" x 4" POST

2" x 6" FACE BOARD SECURE TO 4" x 4" POST W/ 3/8" LAG SCREWS, COUNTERSINK & PLUG END.

2" x 6" DECKING SPACED

CONSTRUCT DECK LEVEL - 8" ABOVE EXG. GRADE.

2" x 6" CAP & FACE ABOVE, CONT. 3 SIDES.

A

A

FRONT EDGE OF BENCH ABOVE

SIMPSON STRONG-TIE "U" SERIES JOIST HANGER

END 2" x 6" CAP & FACE ABOVE

PLAN VIEW

OBSERVATION DECK DTL.

SCALE: 1/2" = 1'-0"

64

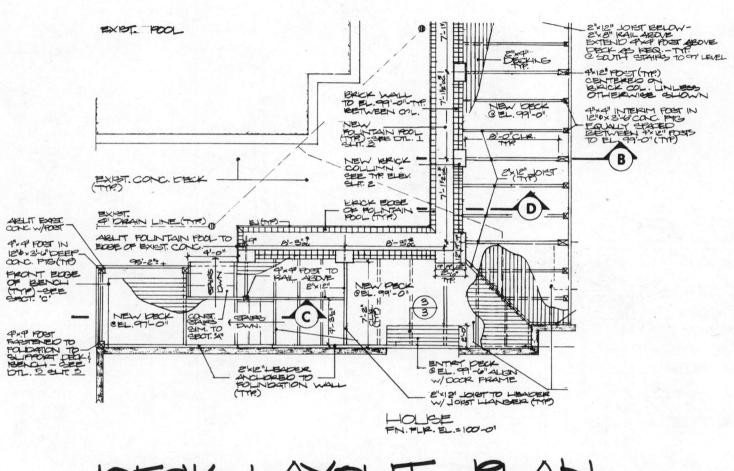

EXIST. POOL

2"x12" JOIST BELOW-
2"x8" RAIL ABOVE
EXTEND 4"x4" POST ABOVE
DECK AS REQ.- TYP.
@ SOUTH STAIRS TO 97' LEVEL

2"x4"
DECKING
TYP.

BRICK WALL
TO EL. 99'-0"-TYP.
BETWEEN COL.

4"x12" POST (TYP.)
CENTERED ON
BRICK COL. UNLESS
OTHERWISE SHOWN

NEW
FOUNTAIN POOL
(TYP.)-SEE DTL. 1
SHT. 3

NEW DECK
@ EL. 99'-0"

4"x4" INTERIM POST IN
12"Ø x 3'-6" CONC. FTG
EQUALLY SPACED
BETWEEN 4"x12" POSTS
TO EL. 99'-0" (TYP.)

EXIST. CONC. DECK
(TYP.)

8'-0" CLR.
TYP.

NEW BRICK
COLUMN -
SEE TYP. ELEV.
SHT. 2

2"x12" JOIST
(TYP.)

Ⓑ

BRICK EDGE
OF FOUNTAIN
POOL (TYP.)

Ⓓ

ALIGN EXIST.
CONC. W/POST

EXIST.
4" DRAIN LINE (TYP.)

EL (TYP.)

4"x4" POST IN
12"Ø x 3'-6" DEEP
CONC. FTG (TYP.)

ALIGN FOUNTAIN POOL TO
EDGE OF EXIST. CONC.

8'-3"±
OC

8'-3"±
OC

FRONT EDGE
OF BENCH
(TYP.)-SEE
SECT. 'C'

95'-2"±

4'-0"

4"x4" POST TO
RAIL ABOVE

NEW DECK
@ EL. 99'-0"

3
3

STAIRS
DWN.

2"x12"

Ⓒ

NEW DECK
@ EL. 97'-0"

CONT.
STAIRS
SIM. TO
SECT. 'C'

STAIRS
DWN.

4"x4" POST
FASTENED TO
FOUNDATION TO
SUPPORT DECK &
BENCH - SEE
DTL. 5 SHT. 5

2"x12" LEADER
ANCHORED TO
FOUNDATION WALL
(TYP.)

ENTRY DECK
@ EL. 99'-6" ALIGN
W/ DOOR FRAME

2"x12" JOIST TO HEADER
W/ JOIST HANGER (TYP.)

HOUSE
FIN. FLR. EL.=100'-0"

DECK LAYOUT PLAN
N.T.S.

65

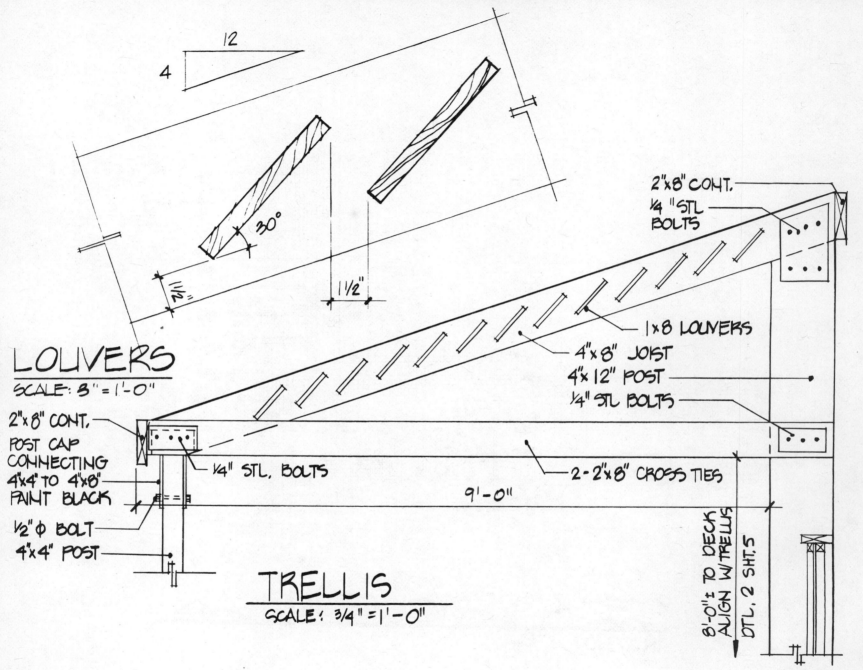

12

4

30°

1 1/2"

1 1/2"

LOUVERS
SCALE: 3" = 1'-0"

2"x8" CONT.

¼" STL BOLTS

1x8 LOUVERS

4"x8" JOIST

4"x12" POST

¼" STL BOLTS

2"x8" CONT.

POST CAP
CONNECTING
4"x4" TO 4"x8"
PAINT BLACK

¼" STL. BOLTS

½" Ø BOLT

4"x4" POST

2-2"x8" CROSS TIES

9'-0"

8'-0"± TO DECK
ALIGN W/ TRELLIS

DTL. 2 SHT. 5

TRELLIS
SCALE: 3/4" = 1'-0"

66

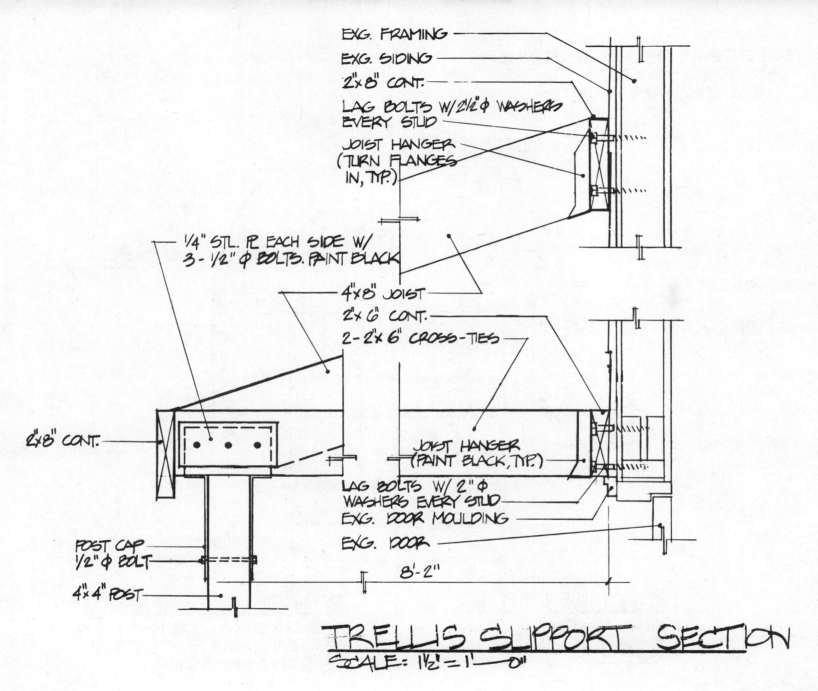

EXG. FRAMING

EXG. SIDING

2"x 8" CONT.

LAG BOLTS W/ 2½" Ø WASHERS
EVERY STUD

JOIST HANGER
(TURN FLANGES
IN, TYP.)

¼" STL. PL. EACH SIDE W/
3 - ½" Ø BOLTS. PAINT BLACK

4"x 8" JOIST

2"x 6" CONT.

2- 2"x 6" CROSS-TIES

2"x 8" CONT.

JOIST HANGER
(PAINT BLACK, TYP.)

LAG BOLTS W/ 2" Ø
WASHERS EVERY STUD

EXG. DOOR MOULDING

EXG. DOOR

POST CAP
½" Ø BOLT

4"x 4" POST

8'-2"

TRELLIS SUPPORT SECTION
SCALE: 1½" = 1'—0"

67

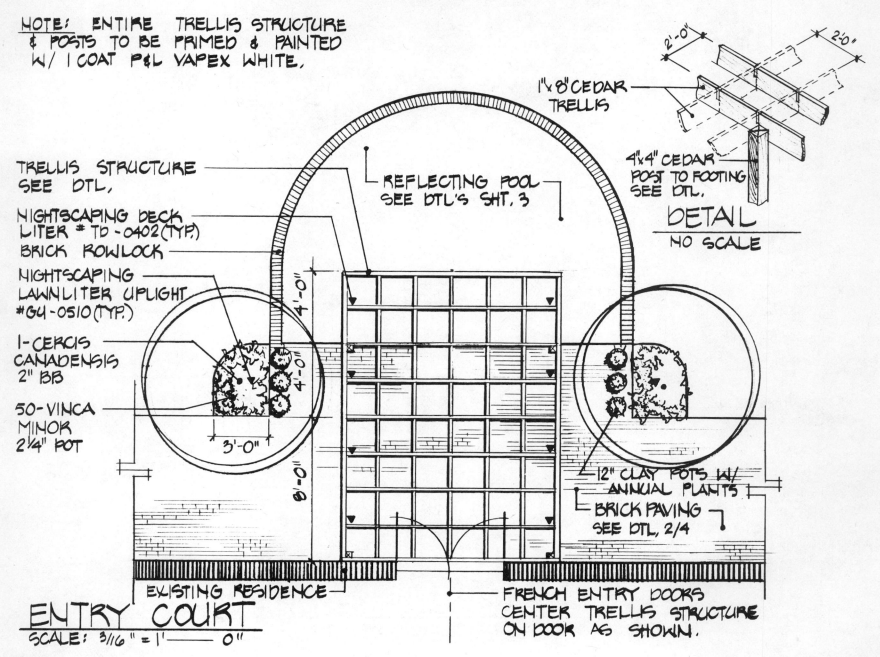

NOTE: ENTIRE TRELLIS STRUCTURE & POSTS TO BE PRIMED & PAINTED W/ 1 COAT P&L VAPEX WHITE.

1"x 8" CEDAR TRELLIS

4"x4" CEDAR POST TO FOOTING SEE DTL.

2'-0"   2'-0"

DETAIL
NO SCALE

TRELLIS STRUCTURE SEE DTL.

NIGHTSCAPING DECK LITER # TD-0402 (TYP.) BRICK ROWLOCK

NIGHTSCAPING LAWNLITER UPLIGHT #GU-0510 (TYP.)

1-CERCIS CANADENSIS 2" BB

50-VINCA MINOR 2¼" POT

REFLECTING POOL SEE DTL'S SHT. 3

4'-0"

4'-0"

3'-0"

8'-0"

12" CLAY POTS W/ ANNUAL PLANTS
BRICK PAVING SEE DTL. 2/4

EXISTING RESIDENCE

FRENCH ENTRY DOORS CENTER TRELLIS STRUCTURE ON DOOR AS SHOWN.

ENTRY COURT
SCALE: 3/16" = 1'——— 0"

68

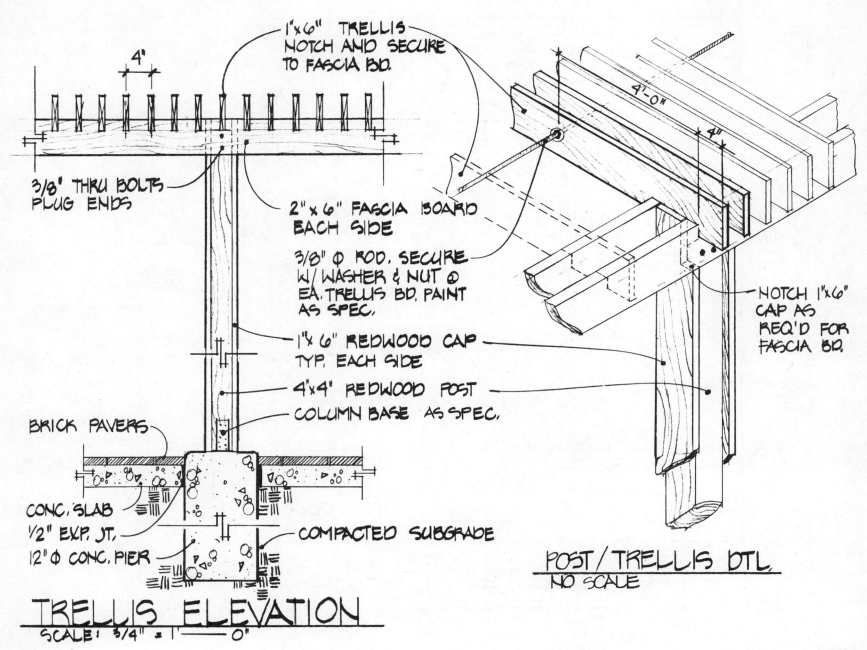

1"x6" TRELLIS
NOTCH AND SECURE
TO FASCIA BD.

4"

3/8" THRU BOLTS
PLUG ENDS

2"x6" FASCIA BOARD
EACH SIDE

3/8" Ø ROD. SECURE
W/ WASHER & NUT @
EA. TRELLIS BD. PAINT
AS SPEC.

1"x6" REDWOOD CAP
TYP. EACH SIDE

4"x4" REDWOOD POST

COLUMN BASE AS SPEC.

BRICK PAVERS

CONC. SLAB
1/2" EXP. JT.
12" Ø CONC. PIER

COMPACTED SUBGRADE

TRELLIS ELEVATION
SCALE: 3/4" = 1'—0"

4'-0"

4"

NOTCH 1"x6"
CAP AS
REQ'D FOR
FASCIA BD.

POST/TRELLIS DTL.
NO SCALE

69

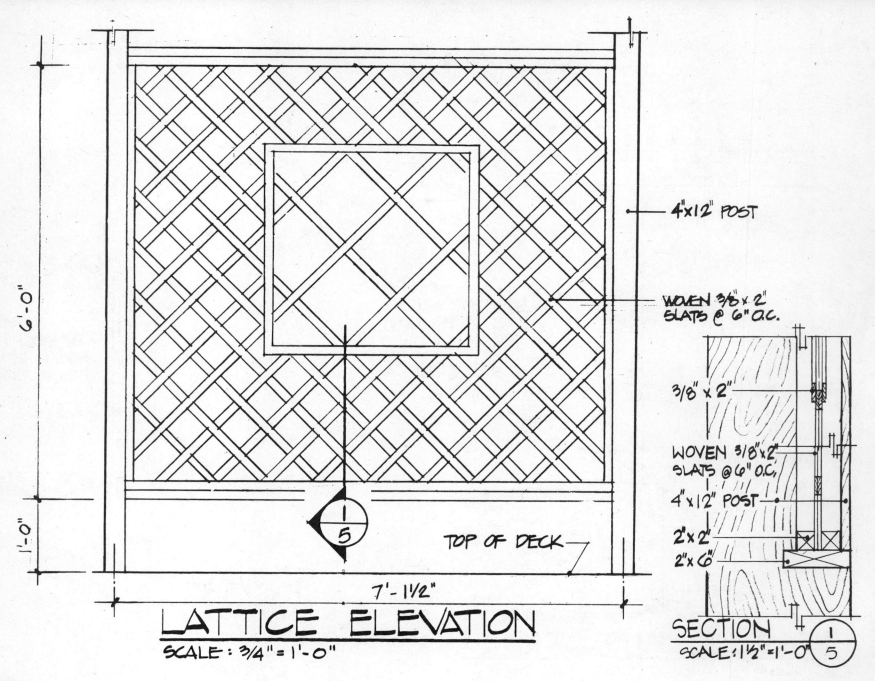

6'-0"

1'-0"

4"x12" POST

WOVEN 3/8" x 2"
SLATS @ 6" O.C.

1
5

TOP OF DECK

7'-1½"

LATTICE ELEVATION
SCALE : 3/4" = 1'-0"

3/8" x 2"

WOVEN 3/8" x 2"
SLATS @ 6" O.C.

4"x12" POST

2"x 2"

2"x 6"

SECTION
SCALE: 1½"=1'-0"

1
5

70

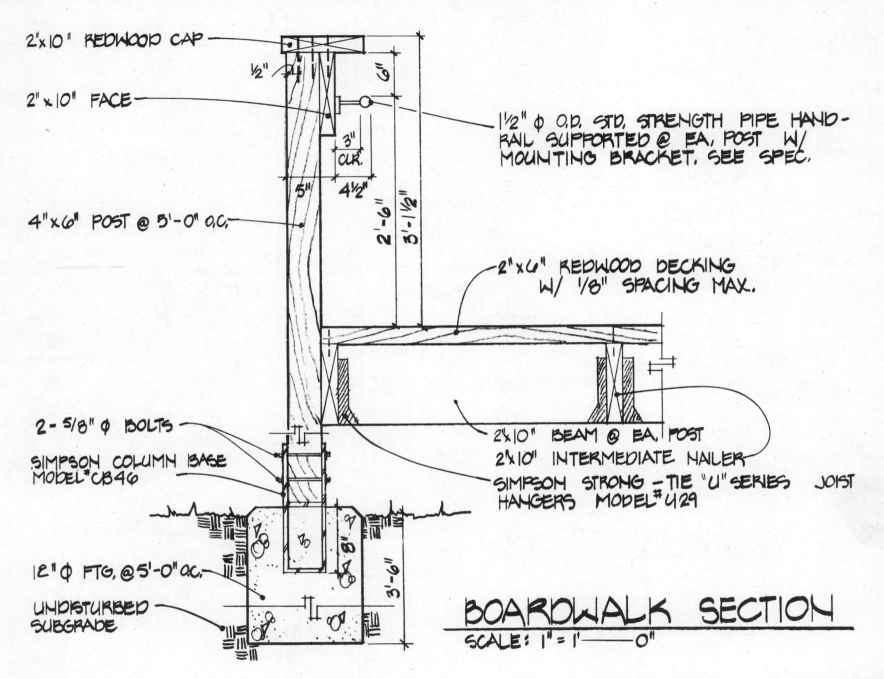

2"x10" REDWOOD CAP

2"x10" FACE

1/2"

6"

1 1/2" Φ O.D. STD. STRENGTH PIPE HAND-
RAIL SUPPORTED @ EA. POST W/
MOUNTING BRACKET. SEE SPEC.

3"
CLR.

5"

4 1/2"

2'-6"

3'-1 1/2"

4"x6" POST @ 5'-0" O.C.

2"x6" REDWOOD DECKING
W/ 1/8" SPACING MAX.

2-5/8" Φ BOLTS

SIMPSON COLUMN BASE
MODEL #CB46

2"x10" BEAM @ EA. POST

2"x10" INTERMEDIATE NAILER

SIMPSON STRONG-TIE "U" SERIES JOIST
HANGERS MODEL #U29

3'

8"

12" Φ FTG. @ 5'-0" O.C.

3'-6"

UNDISTURBED
SUBGRADE

BOARDWALK SECTION
SCALE: 1" = 1'————0"

71

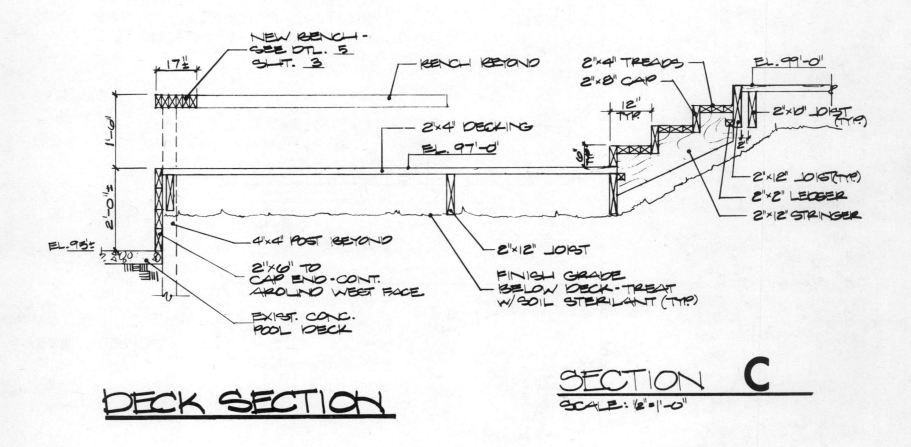

NEW BENCH -
SEE DTL. 5
SHT. 3

BENCH BEYOND

2"x4" TREADS

2"x8" CAP

EL. 99'-0"

17±

2"x4" DECKING

EL. 97'-0"

12"
TYP.

2"x6" JOIST
(TYP.)

1'-0"

2"x12" JOIST (TYP.)

2"x2" LEDGER

2"x12" STRINGER

2'-0"±

4"x4" POST BEYOND

2"x12" JOIST

EL. 95±

2"x6" TO
CAP END-CONT.
AROUND WEST FACE

FINISH GRADE
BELOW DECK-TREAT
W/ SOIL STERILANT (TYP.)

EXIST. CONC.
POOL DECK

DECK SECTION

SECTION C

SCALE: 1/2"=1'-0"

72

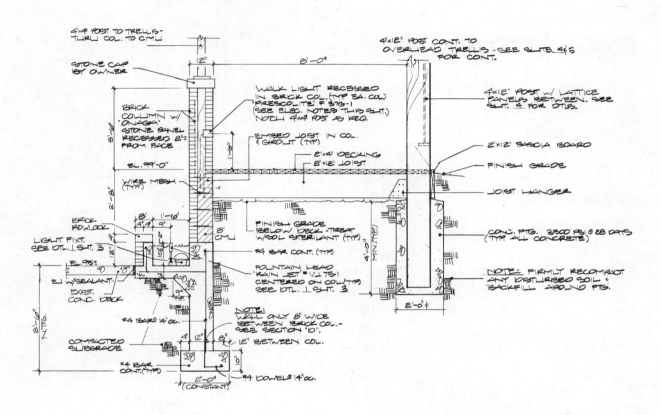

4"x4" POST TO TRELLIS-
THRU COL. TO CMU

STONE CAP
BY OWNER

BRICK
COLUMN W/
"ONAGA"
STONE PANEL
RECESSED 2"
FROM FACE

EL.99'-0"

WIRE MESH
(TYP)

BRICK
ROWLOCK

LIGHT FIXT.
SEE DTL. 1 SHT. 3

EL.95'-0"

EL. W/SEALANT-
EXIST.
CONC. DECK

COMPACTED
SUBGRADE

#4 BARS 14" OC.

#4 BAR
CONT.(TYP)

2'-0"
(CONSTANT)

#4 DOWELS 14" OC.

12"

4' 4"   9"

8"

2"   2"

8"
CMU

4"   12"   8"   12" BETWEEN COL.

WALK LIGHT RECESSED
IN BRICK COL. (TYP EA. COL)
"PRESCOLITE" # 378-1
(SEE ELEC. NOTES THIS SHT.)
NOTCH 4"x4" POST AS REQ.

EMBED JOIST IN COL.
& GROUT (TYP)

2"x4" DECKING
2"x12" JOIST

FINISH GRADE
BELOW DECK-TREAT
W/SOIL STERILANT (TYP)

#4 BAR CONT. (TYP)

FOUNTAIN HEAD
"RAIN JET" # VJ 75-1
CENTERED ON COL. (TYP)
SEE DTL. 1 SHT. 3

NOTE:
WALL ONLY 8" WIDE
BETWEEN BRICK COL.-
SEE SECTION "D".

4"x12" POST CONT. TO
OVERHEAD TRELLIS - SEE SHTS. 4 & 5
FOR CONT.

4"x12" POST W/ LATTICE
PANELS BETWEEN. SEE
SHT. 4 FOR DTLS.

2"x12" FASCIA BOARD

FINISH GRADE

JOIST HANGER

CONC. FTG. 3300 PSI @ 28 DAYS
(TYP. ALL CONCRETE)

NOTE: FIRMLY RECOMPACT
ANY DISTURBED SOIL &
BACKFILL AROUND FTG.

2'-0" Ø

8'-0"
2'-8"
8'-0"
N.T.S.
4'-0" MIN. (TYP)
8'-0"
12"

SECTION @ DECK @ FOUNTAIN
SCALE: ¼" = 1'————0"

73

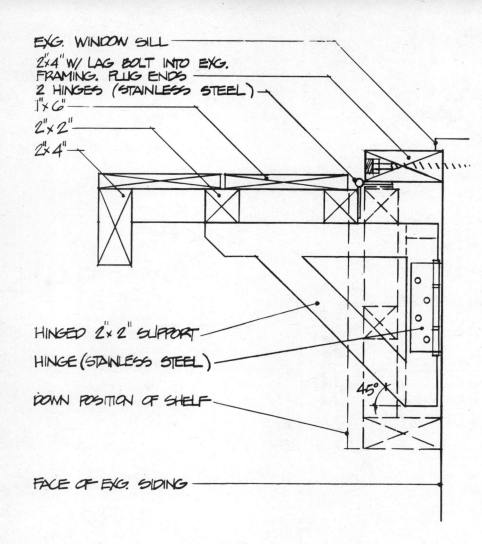

EXG. WINDOW SILL

2"×4" W/ LAG BOLT INTO EXG. FRAMING. PLUG ENDS

2 HINGES (STAINLESS STEEL)

1"×6"

2"×2"

2"×4"

HINGED 2"×2" SUPPORT

HINGE (STAINLESS STEEL)

DOWN POSITION OF SHELF

45°

FACE OF EXG. SIDING

SHELF DETAIL
SCALE : 3" = 1'-0"

(3 / 5)

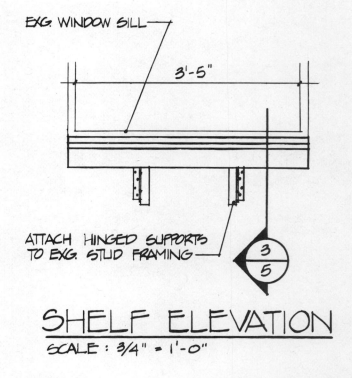

EXG. WINDOW SILL

3'-5"

ATTACH HINGED SUPPORTS TO EXG. STUD FRAMING

(3 / 5)

SHELF ELEVATION
SCALE : 3/4" = 1'-0"

74

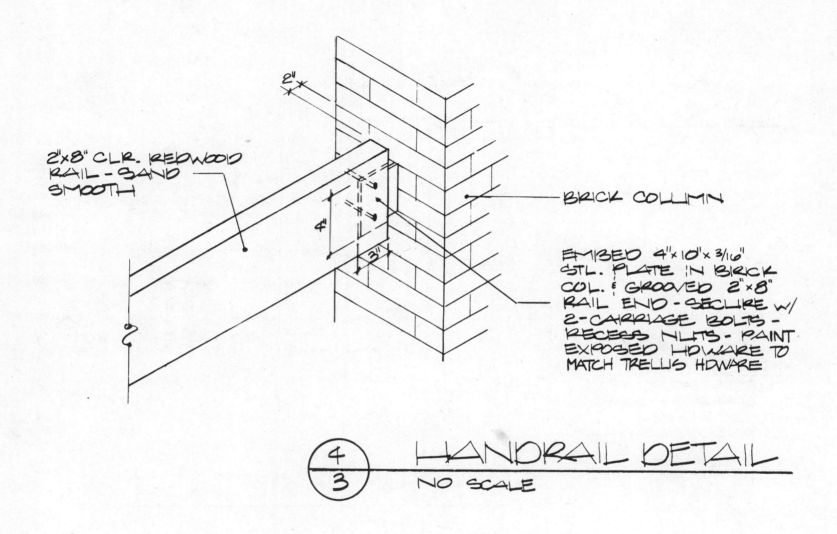

2"x8" CLR. REDWOOD
RAIL - SAND
SMOOTH

2"

4"

3"

BRICK COLUMN

EMBED 4"x10'x3/16"
STL. PLATE IN BRICK
COL. & GROOVED 2"x8"
RAIL END - SECURE w/
2-CARRIAGE BOLTS -
RECESS NUTS - PAINT
EXPOSED HDWARE TO
MATCH TRELLIS HDWARE

$\frac{4}{3}$ HANDRAIL DETAIL
NO SCALE

75

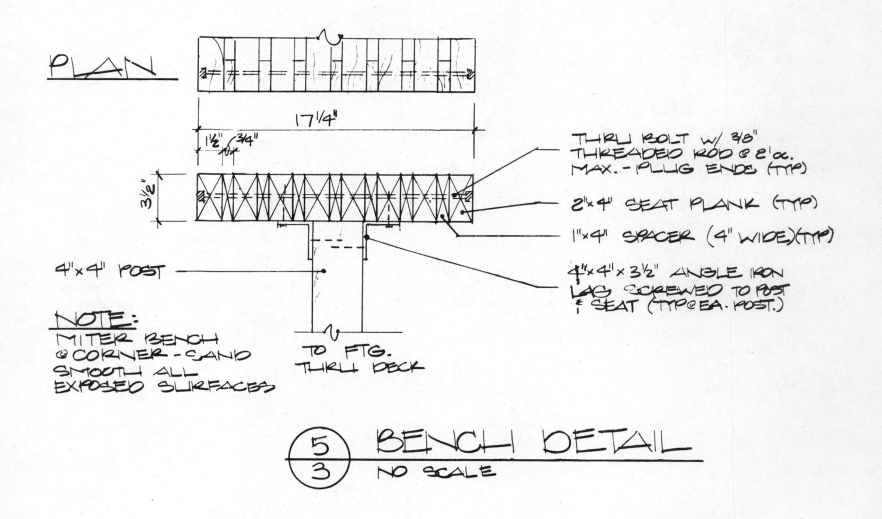

PLAN

17 1/4"

1 1/2" 3/4"

3 1/2"

THRU BOLT w/ 3/8"
THREADED ROD @ 2' o.c.
MAX. - PLUG ENDS (TYP)

2"x4" SEAT PLANK (TYP)

1"x4" SPACER (4" WIDE)(TYP)

4"x4" POST

4"x4"x3 1/2" ANGLE IRON
LAG SCREWED TO POST
& SEAT (TYP @ EA. POST.)

NOTE:
MITER BENCH
@ CORNER - SAND
SMOOTH ALL
EXPOSED SURFACES

TO FTG.
THRU DECK

5/3 BENCH DETAIL
NO SCALE

76

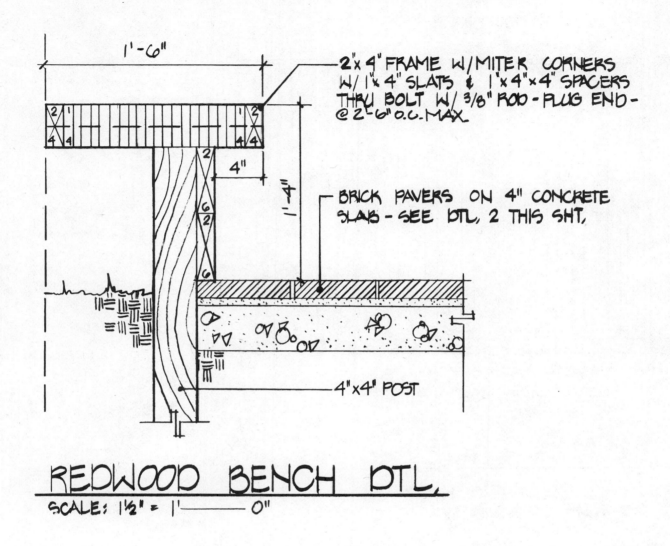

1'-6"

2"x 4" FRAME W/MITER CORNERS
W/ 1"x 4" SLATS & 1"x 4"x 4" SPACERS
THRU BOLT W/ 3/8" ROD - PLUG END -
@ 2'-6" O.C. MAX.

4"

1'-4"

BRICK PAVERS ON 4" CONCRETE
SLAB - SEE DTL. 2 THIS SHT.

4"x4" POST

REDWOOD BENCH DTL.
SCALE: 1½" = 1'———— 0"

77

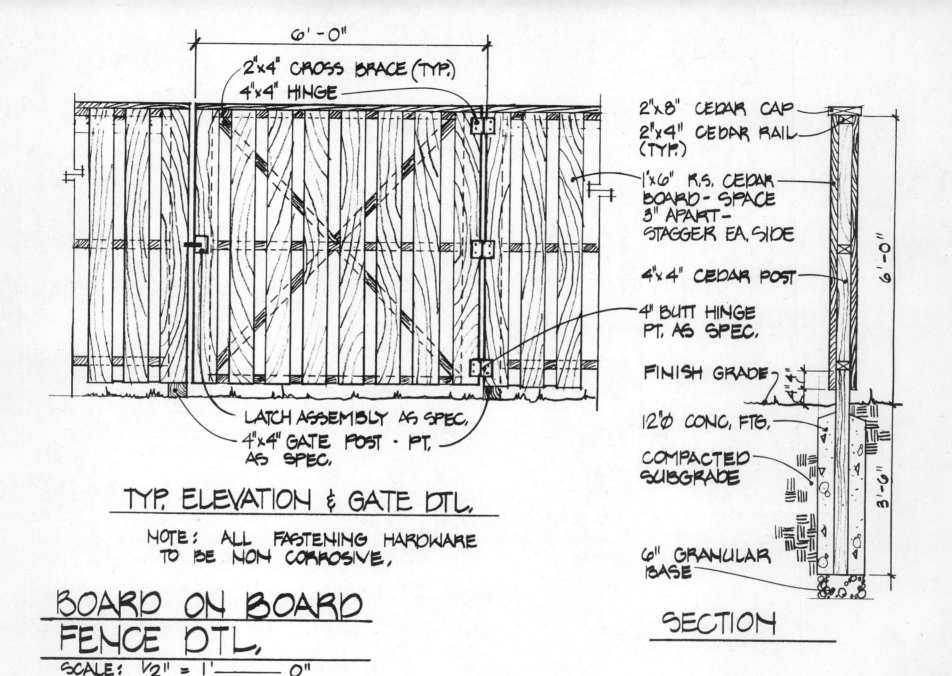

6'-0"

2"x4" CROSS BRACE (TYP.)

4"x4" HINGE

2"x8" CEDAR CAP

2"x4" CEDAR RAIL (TYP.)

1"x6" R.S. CEDAR BOARD - SPACE 3" APART - STAGGER EA. SIDE

4"x4" CEDAR POST

4" BUTT HINGE PT. AS SPEC.

FINISH GRADE

12"Ø CONC. FTG.

COMPACTED SUBGRADE

6" GRANULAR BASE

LATCH ASSEMBLY AS SPEC.

4"x4" GATE POST - PT. AS SPEC.

6'-0"

3'-6"

TYP. ELEVATION & GATE DTL.

NOTE: ALL FASTENING HARDWARE TO BE NON CORROSIVE.

BOARD ON BOARD FENCE DTL.

SCALE: ½" = 1'——— 0"

SECTION

78

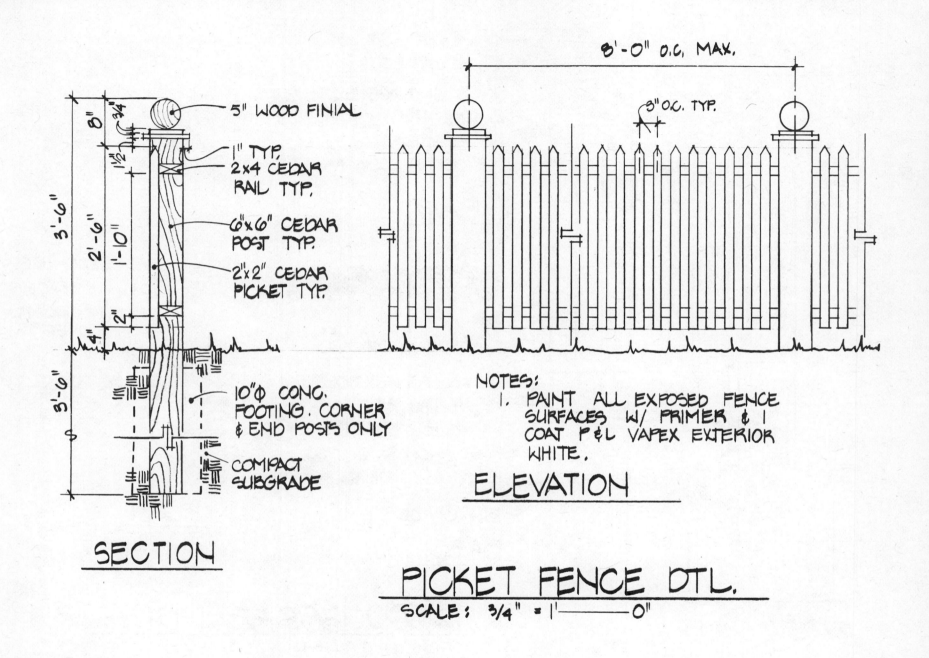

5" WOOD FINIAL

1" TYP.
2×4 CEDAR
RAIL TYP.

6"×6" CEDAR
POST TYP.

2"×2" CEDAR
PICKET TYP.

10"Ø CONC.
FOOTING. CORNER
& END POSTS ONLY

COMPACT
SUBGRADE

SECTION

8'-0" O.C. MAX.

3" O.C. TYP.

NOTES:
1. PAINT ALL EXPOSED FENCE
   SURFACES W/ PRIMER & 1
   COAT P&L VAPEX EXTERIOR
   WHITE.

ELEVATION

PICKET FENCE DTL.
SCALE: 3/4" = 1'———0"

79

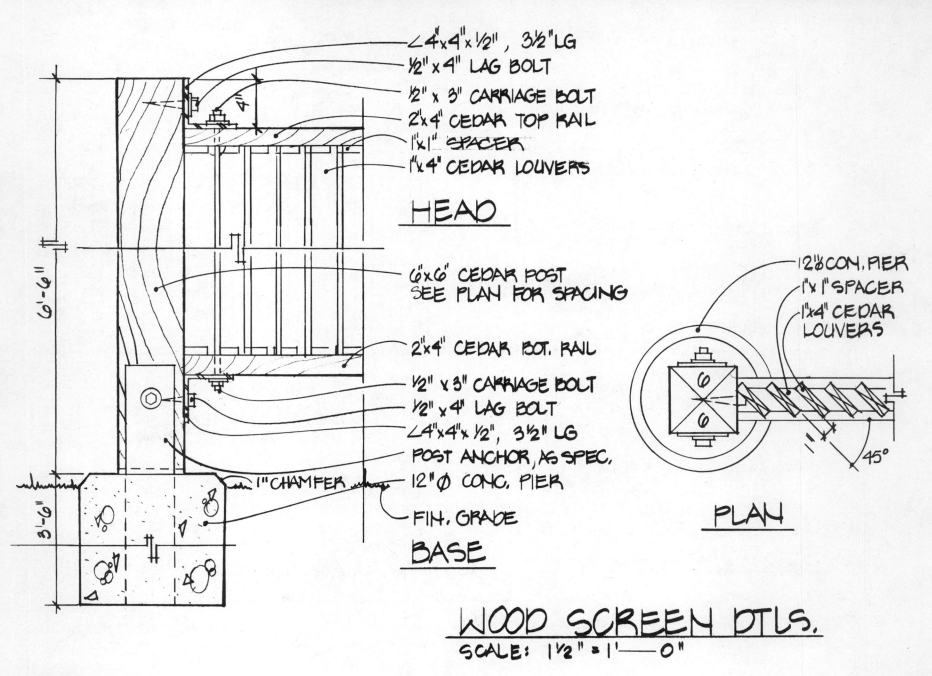

∠4"x4"x½", 3½"LG
½"x4" LAG BOLT
½"x3" CARRIAGE BOLT
2"x4" CEDAR TOP RAIL
1"x1" SPACER
1"x4" CEDAR LOUVERS

HEAD

6"x6" CEDAR POST
SEE PLAN FOR SPACING

2"x4" CEDAR BOT. RAIL

½"x3" CARRIAGE BOLT
½"x4" LAG BOLT
∠4"x4"x½", 3½"LG
POST ANCHOR, AS SPEC.
12"Ø CONC. PIER
1"CHAMFER
FIN. GRADE

BASE

6'-6"

3'-6"

12"Ø CON. PIER
1"x1" SPACER
1"x4" CEDAR LOUVERS

6
6

45°

PLAN

WOOD SCREEN DTLS.
SCALE: 1½" = 1'——0"

80

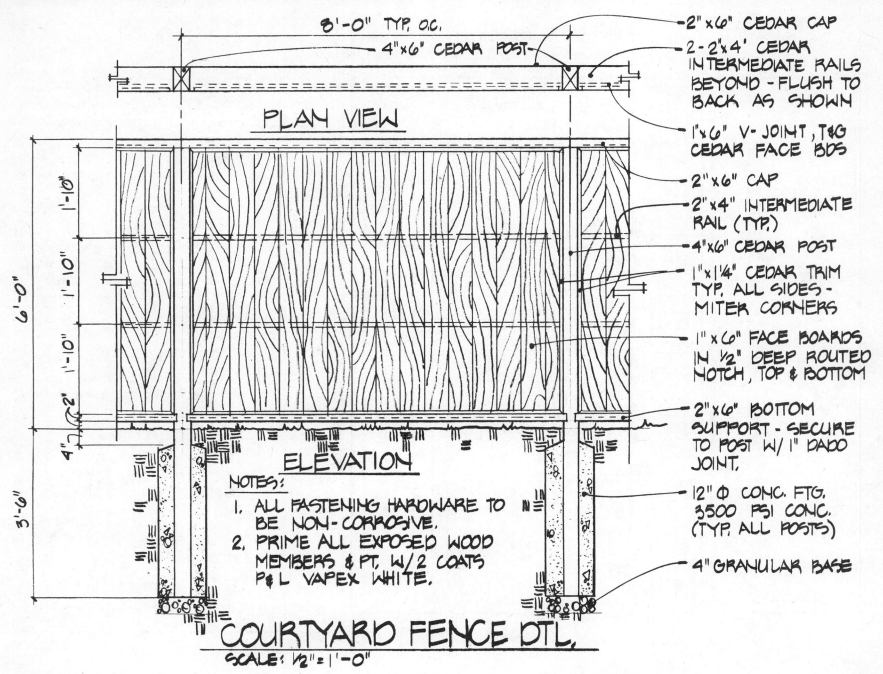

PLAN VIEW

ELEVATION

NOTES:
1. ALL FASTENING HARDWARE TO BE NON-CORROSIVE.
2. PRIME ALL EXPOSED WOOD MEMBERS & PT. W/ 2 COATS P&L VAPEX WHITE.

COURTYARD FENCE DTL.

SCALE: ½" = 1'-0"

8'-0" TYP. O.C.

4"×6" CEDAR POST

1'-0"
1'-10"
1'-10"
1'-10"
6'-0"
2"
4"
3'-6"

2"×6" CEDAR CAP

2-2"×4" CEDAR INTERMEDIATE RAILS BEYOND - FLUSH TO BACK AS SHOWN

1"×6" V-JOINT, T&G CEDAR FACE BDS

2"×6" CAP

2"×4" INTERMEDIATE RAIL (TYP.)

4"×6" CEDAR POST

1"×1¼" CEDAR TRIM TYP. ALL SIDES - MITER CORNERS

1"×6" FACE BOARDS IN ½" DEEP ROUTED NOTCH, TOP & BOTTOM

2"×6" BOTTOM SUPPORT - SECURE TO POST W/ 1" DADO JOINT.

12" Ø CONC. FTG. 3500 PSI CONC. (TYP. ALL POSTS)

4" GRANULAR BASE

81

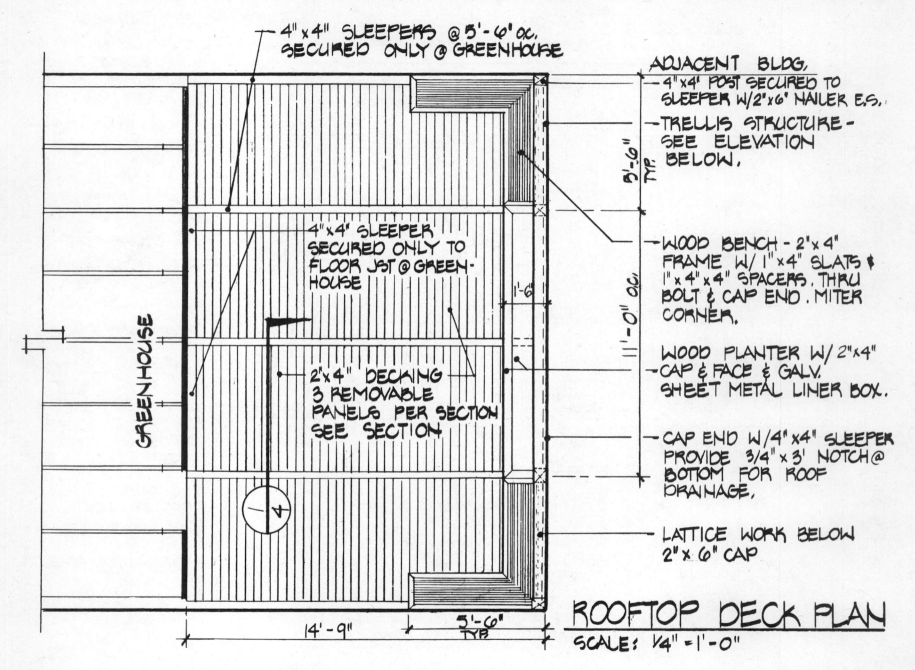

4" x 4" SLEEPERS @ 5'-6' O.C.
SECURED ONLY @ GREENHOUSE

ADJACENT BLDG.

4" x 4" POST SECURED TO
SLEEPER W/ 2"x6" NAILER E.S.

TRELLIS STRUCTURE -
SEE ELEVATION
BELOW.

4" x 4" SLEEPER
SECURED ONLY TO
FLOOR JST @ GREEN-
HOUSE

GREENHOUSE

5'-6" TYP

11'-0" O.C.

1'-6"

WOOD BENCH - 2"x4"
FRAME W/ 1"x4" SLATS &
1"x 4"x 4" SPACERS. THRU
BOLT & CAP END. MITER
CORNER.

2"x4" DECKING
3 REMOVABLE
PANELS PER SECTION
SEE SECTION

WOOD PLANTER W/ 2"x4"
CAP & FACE & GALV.
SHEET METAL LINER BOX.

CAP END W/ 4"x4" SLEEPER
PROVIDE 3/4" x 3' NOTCH @
BOTTOM FOR ROOF
DRAINAGE.

LATTICE WORK BELOW
2" x 6" CAP

14'-9"

5'-6"
TYP

ROOFTOP DECK PLAN
SCALE: 1/4" = 1'-0"

82

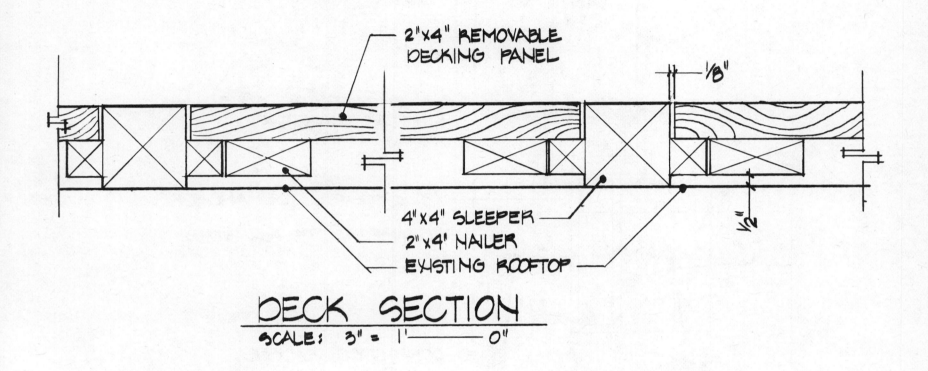

2"x4" REMOVABLE
DECKING PANEL

1/8"

4"x4" SLEEPER

2"x4" NAILER

EXISTING ROOFTOP

1/2"

DECK SECTION
SCALE: 3" = 1'———— 0"

83

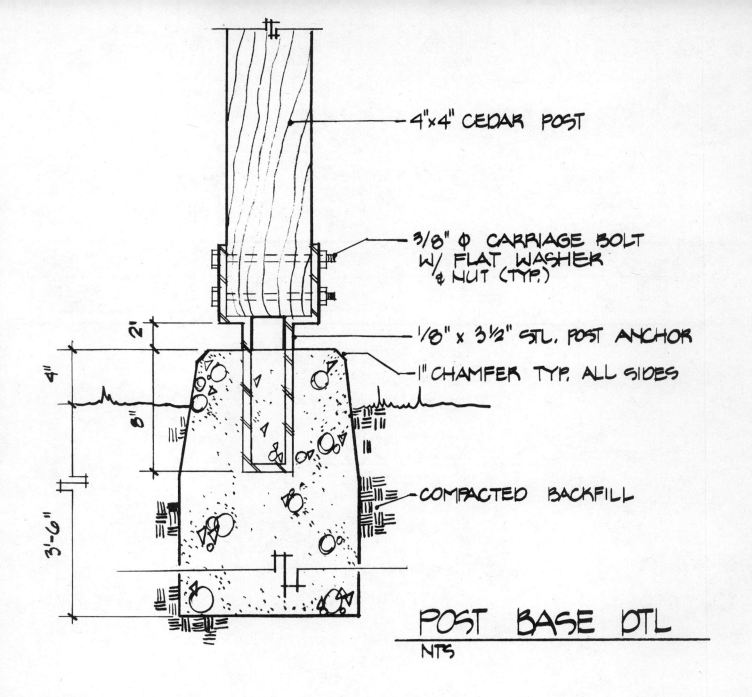

4"x4" CEDAR POST

3/8" Ø CARRIAGE BOLT
W/ FLAT WASHER
& NUT (TYP.)

1/8" x 3½" STL. POST ANCHOR

1" CHAMFER TYP. ALL SIDES

COMPACTED BACKFILL

2"

4"

8"

3'-6"

POST BASE DTL
NTS

84

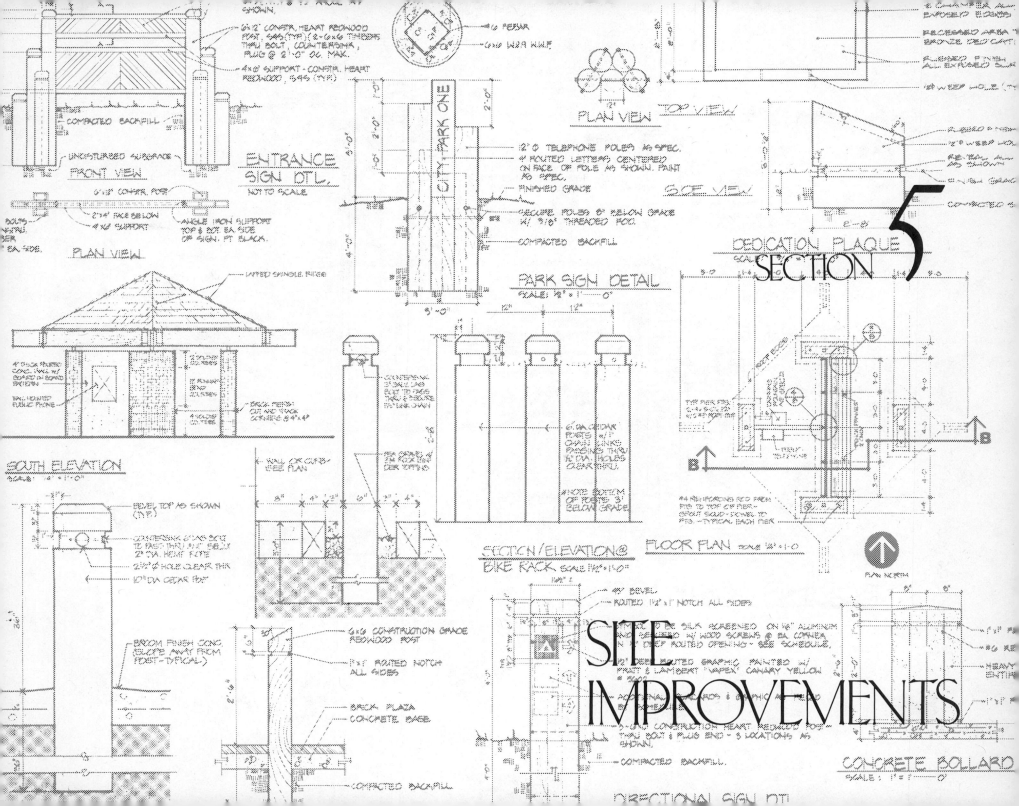

SITE
IMPROVEMENTS

SECTION 5

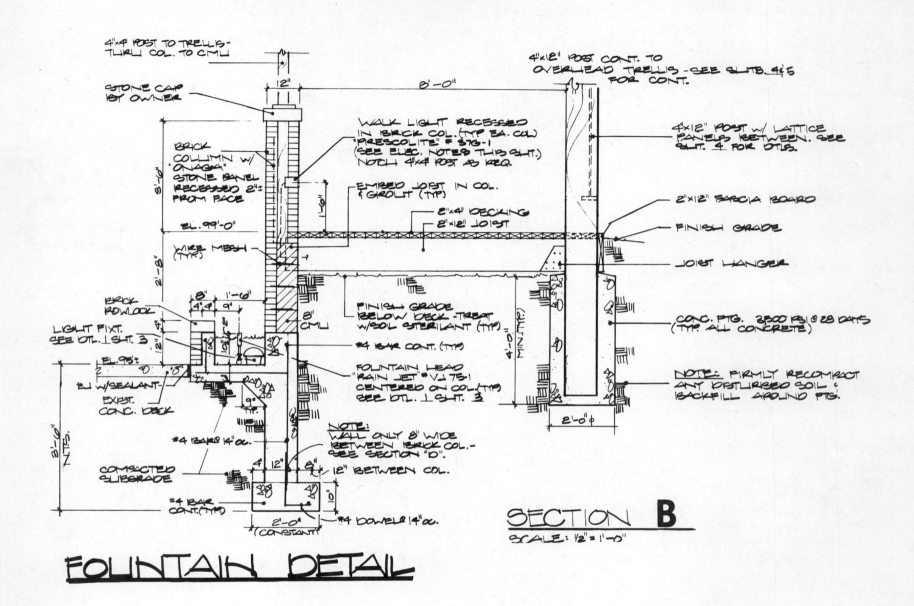

4"x4" POST TO TRELLIS—
THRU COL. TO CMU

STONE CAP
BY OWNER

BRICK
COLUMN W/
"ONAGA"
STONE PANEL
RECESSED 2"±
FROM FACE

EL.99'-0"

WIRE MESH
(TYP.)

BRICK
ROWLOCK

LIGHT FIXT.
SEE DTL. 1 SHT. 3

EL.95'±

EL.W/SEALANT
EXIST.
CONC. DECK

COMPACTED
SUBGRADE

#4 BARS 14" O.C.

#4 BAR
CONT.(TYP)

2'-0"
(CONSTANT)

#4 DOWEL 14" O.C.

WALK LIGHT RECESSED
IN BRICK COL. (TYP EA. COL)
"PRESCOLITE" #378-1
(SEE ELEC. NOTES THIS SHT.)
NOTCH 4"x4" POST AS REQ.

EMBED JOIST IN COL.
& GROUT (TYP)

2"x4" DECKING
2"x12" JOIST

FINISH GRADE
BELOW DECK-TREAT
W/SOIL STERILANT (TYP)

#4 BAR CONT. (TYP)

FOUNTAIN HEAD
"RAIN JET" #VJ 75-1
CENTERED ON COL. (TYP)
SEE DTL. 1 SHT. 3

NOTE:
WALL ONLY 8" WIDE
BETWEEN BRICK COL.-
SEE SECTION "D".

12" BETWEEN COL.

8"
CMU

4"x12" POST CONT. TO
OVERHEAD TRELLIS-SEE SHTS. 4&5
FOR CONT.

4"x12" POST W/ LATTICE
PANELS BETWEEN. SEE
SHT. 4 FOR DTLS.

2"x12" FASCIA BOARD

FINISH GRADE

JOIST HANGER

CONC. FTG. 3500 PSI @ 28 DAYS
(TYP. ALL CONCRETE)

NOTE: FIRMLY RECOMPACT
ANY DISTURBED SOIL &
BACKFILL AROUND FTG.

2'-0"Ø

SECTION B
SCALE: 1/2" = 1'-0"

FOUNTAIN DETAIL

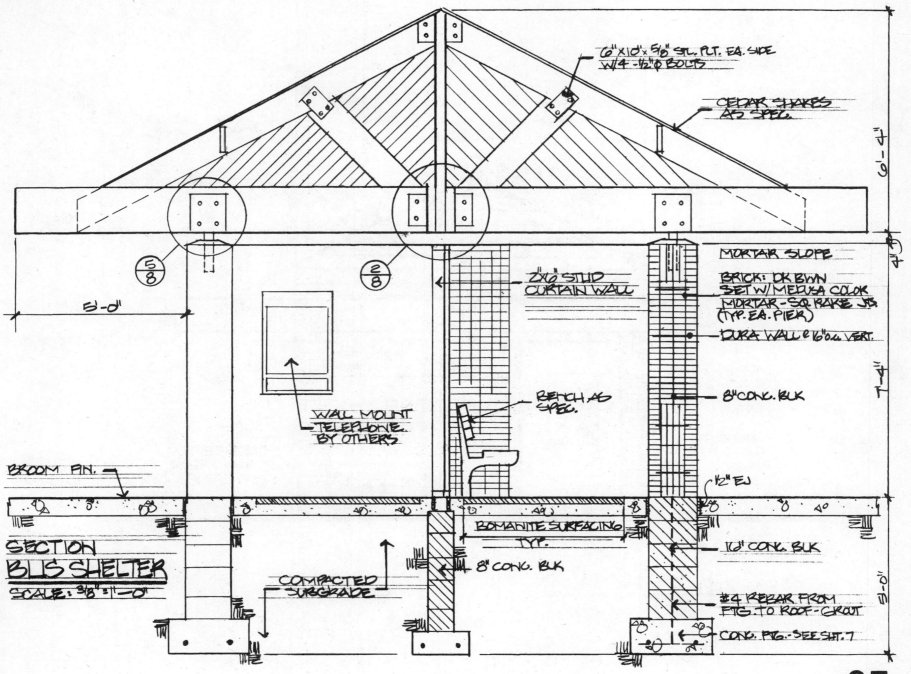

6"x10"x 5/8" STL. PLT. EA. SIDE
w/4 -1/2"Ø BOLTS

CEDAR SHAKES
AS SPEC.

MORTAR SLOPE

BRICK: DK BWN
SET w/ MEDUSA COLOR
MORTAR - SQ. RAKE JTS.
(TYP. EA. PIER)

DURA WALL @ 16"O.C. VERT.

2x6 STUD
CURTAIN WALL

8" CONC. BLK

5/8

2/8

WALL MOUNT
TELEPHONE.
BY OTHERS

BENCH AS
SPEC.

1/2" EJ

BROOM FIN.

BOMANITE SURFACING
TYP.

16" CONC. BLK

SECTION
BUS SHELTER
SCALE: 3/8" = 1'-0"

COMPACTED
SUBGRADE

8" CONC. BLK

#4 REBAR FROM
FTG. TO ROOF-GROUT

CONC. FTG.-SEE SHT. 7

5'-0"

9'-1"

4'-3"

7'-1"

5'-0"

87

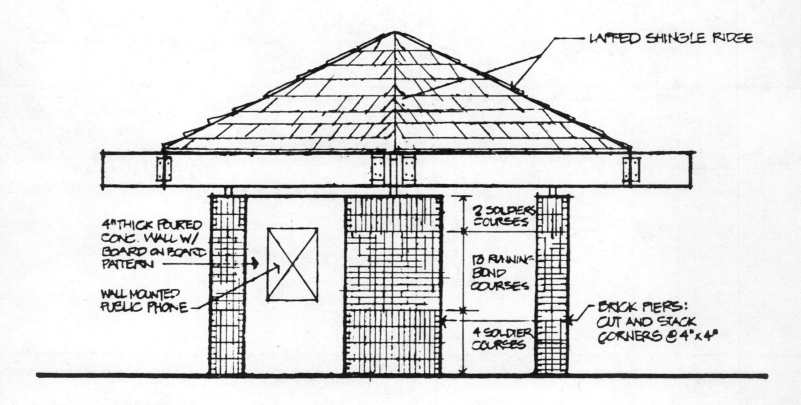

LAPPED SHINGLE RIDGE

4" THICK POURED
CONC. WALL W/
BOARD ON BOARD
PATTERN

WALL MOUNTED
PUBLIC PHONE

2 SOLDIER
COURSES

13 RUNNING-
BOND
COURSES

4 SOLDIER
COURSES

BRICK PIERS:
CUT AND STACK
CORNERS @ 4" x 4"

SOUTH ELEVATION
SCALE: 1/4" = 1'-0"

88

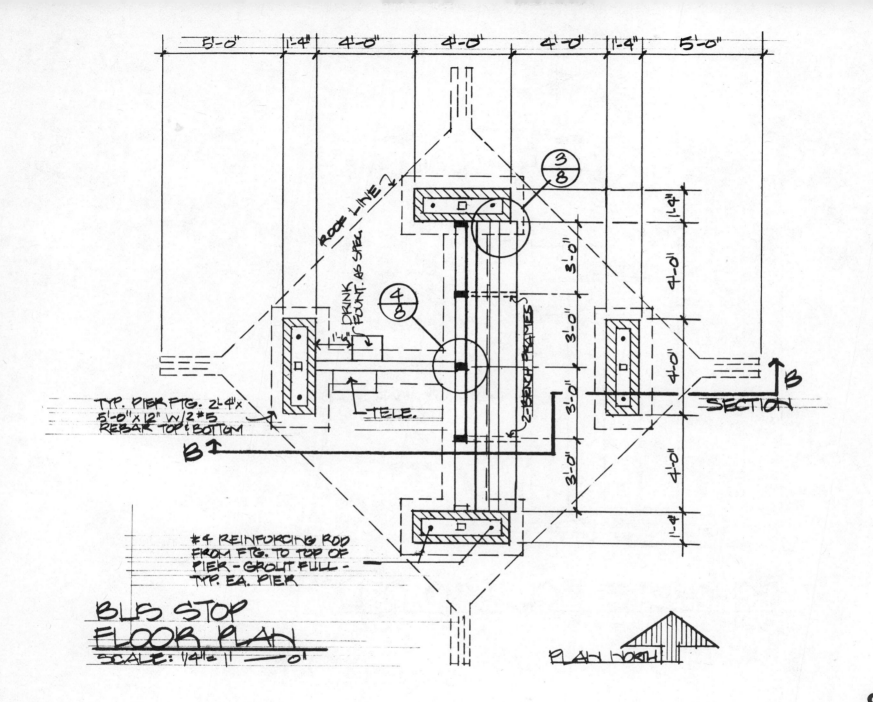

5'-0"   1'-4"   4'-0"   4'-0"   4'-0"   1'-4"   5'-0"

ROOF LINE

3/8

DRINK FOUNT. AS SPEC.

4/8

1'-4"

4'-0"

3'-0"

3'-0"

2-BENCH FRAMES

3'-0"

4'-0"

SECTION

B

3'-0"

TELE.

TYP. PIER FTG. 2'-4" x
5'-0" x 12" W/2 #5
REBAR TOP & BOTTOM

B

4'-0"

3'-0"

1'-4"

#4 REINFORCING ROD
FROM FTG. TO TOP OF
PIER - GROUT FULL -
TYP. EA. PIER

BUS STOP
FLOOR PLAN
SCALE: 1/4" = 1'-0"

PLAN NORTH

89

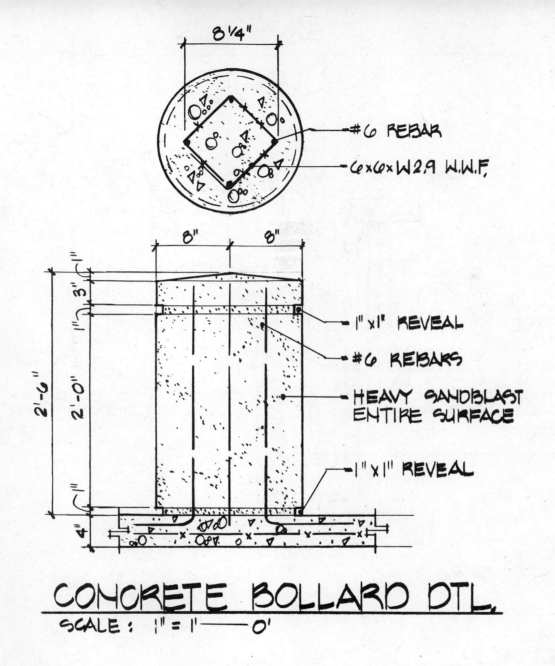

8¼"

#6 REBAR

6×6×W2.9 W.W.F.

8"   8"

1"

3"

1"

2'-0"

2'-6"

1"

4"

1"×1" REVEAL

#6 REBARS

HEAVY SANDBLAST
ENTIRE SURFACE

1"×1" REVEAL

CONCRETE BOLLARD DTL.
SCALE : 1" = 1'———— 0'

90

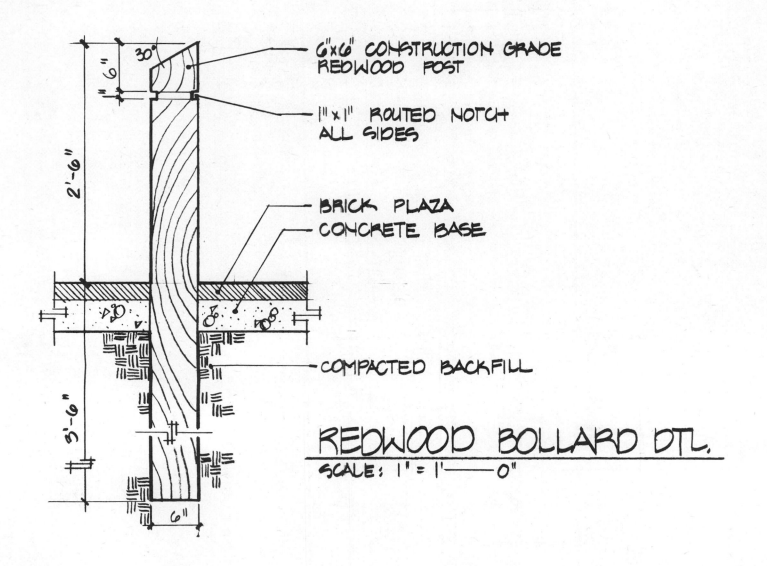

6"x6" CONSTRUCTION GRADE
REDWOOD POST

1"x1" ROUTED NOTCH
ALL SIDES

BRICK PLAZA
CONCRETE BASE

COMPACTED BACKFILL

30°

6"

2'-6"

3'-6"

6"

REDWOOD BOLLARD DTL.
SCALE: 1" = 1'———0"

91

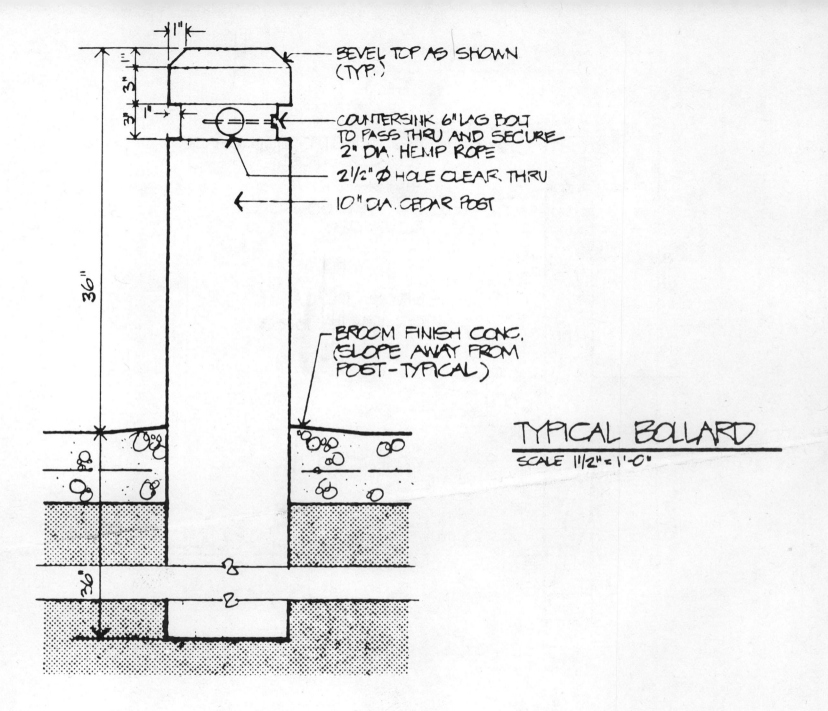

BEVEL TOP AS SHOWN
(TYP.)

COUNTERSINK 6" LAG BOLT
TO PASS THRU AND SECURE
2" DIA. HEMP ROPE

2½" Ø HOLE CLEAR. THRU

10" DIA. CEDAR POST

BROOM FINISH CONC.
(SLOPE AWAY FROM
POST - TYPICAL)

1"

3"

3" 1"

36"

36"

TYPICAL BOLLARD
SCALE 1½" = 1'-0"

92

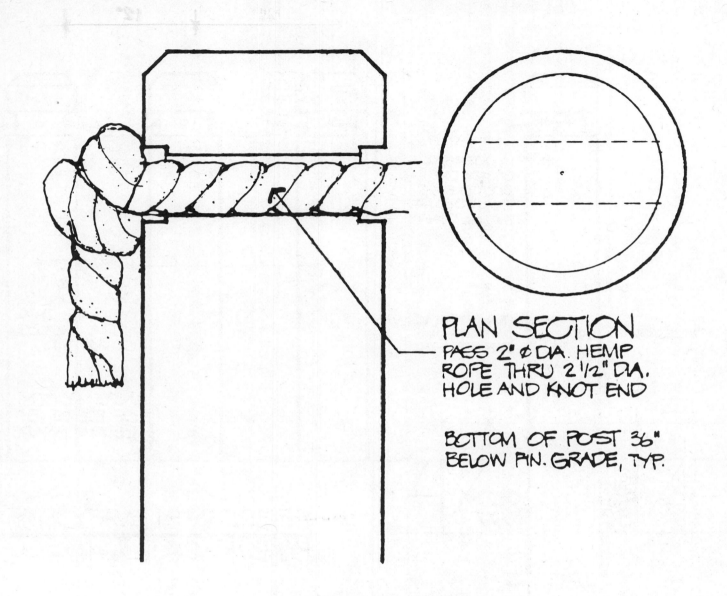

PLAN SECTION
PASS 2" ∅ DIA. HEMP
ROPE THRU 2 1/2" DIA.
HOLE AND KNOT END

BOTTOM OF POST 36"
BELOW FIN. GRADE, TYP.

BOLLARD END POST
SCALE 3" = 1'-0"

93

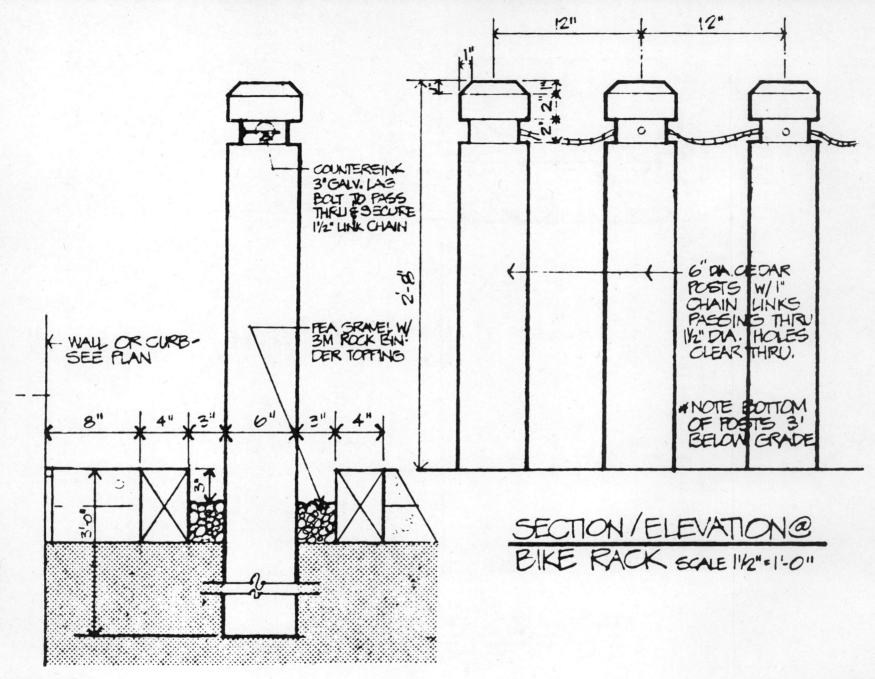

COUNTERSINK
3" GALV. LAG
BOLT TO PASS
THRU & SECURE
1½" LINK CHAIN

PEA GRAVEL W/
3M ROCK BIN-
DER TOPPING

WALL OR CURB-
SEE PLAN

2'-8"

8"   4"   3"   6"   3"   4"

3'-0"

3"

12"   12"

1"

2' 2"

6" DIA. CEDAR
POSTS W/ 1"
CHAIN LINKS
PASSING THRU
1½" DIA. HOLES
CLEAR THRU.

* NOTE BOTTOM
OF POSTS 3'
BELOW GRADE

SECTION / ELEVATION @
BIKE RACK SCALE 1½" = 1'-0"

94

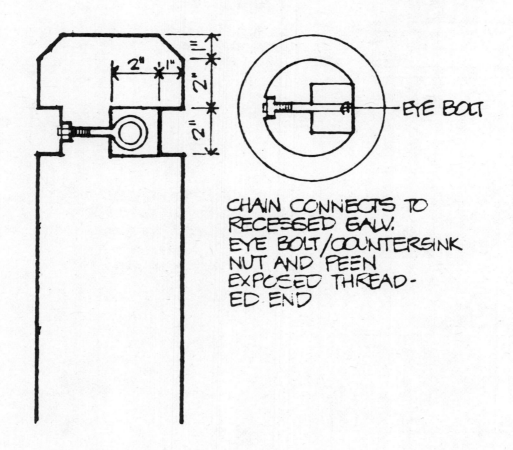

2"

2"

2"

1"

EYE BOLT

CHAIN CONNECTS TO
RECESSED GALV.
EYE BOLT/COUNTERSINK
NUT AND PEEN
EXPOSED THREAD-
ED END

END POST @ BIKE RACK
SCALE 3"=1'-0"

95

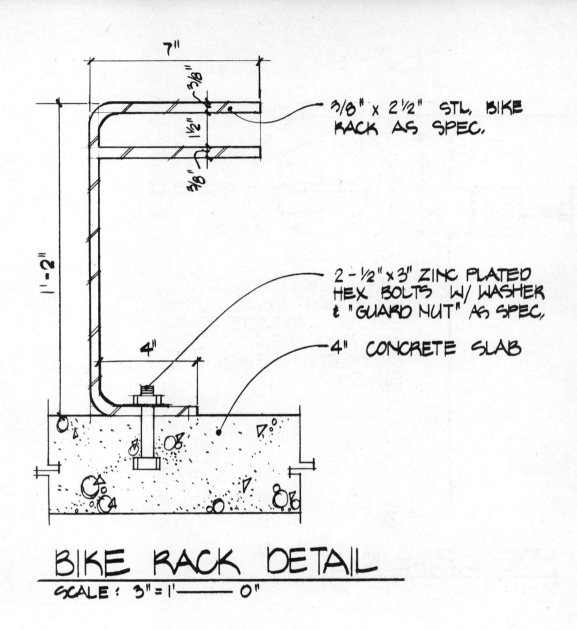

7"

3/8"

1½"

3/8"

1'-2"

4"

3/8" x 2½" STL, BIKE
RACK AS SPEC.

2 - ½" x 3" ZINC PLATED
HEX BOLTS W/ WASHER
& "GUARD NUT" AS SPEC,

4" CONCRETE SLAB

BIKE RACK DETAIL
SCALE: 3" = 1'———— 0"

96

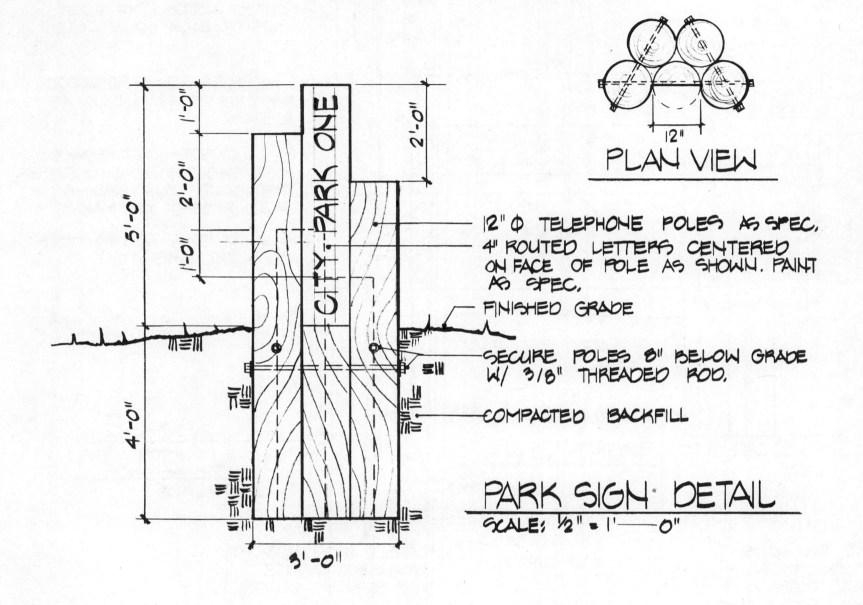

PLAN VIEW

12" Ø TELEPHONE POLES AS SPEC.

4" ROUTED LETTERS CENTERED ON FACE OF POLE AS SHOWN. PAINT AS SPEC.

FINISHED GRADE

SECURE POLES 8" BELOW GRADE W/ 3/8" THREADED ROD.

COMPACTED BACKFILL

CITY PARK ONE

12"

1'-0"
2'-0"
1'-0"
5'-0"
2'-0"
4'-0"
3'-0"

PARK SIGN DETAIL
SCALE: ½" = 1'—0"

97

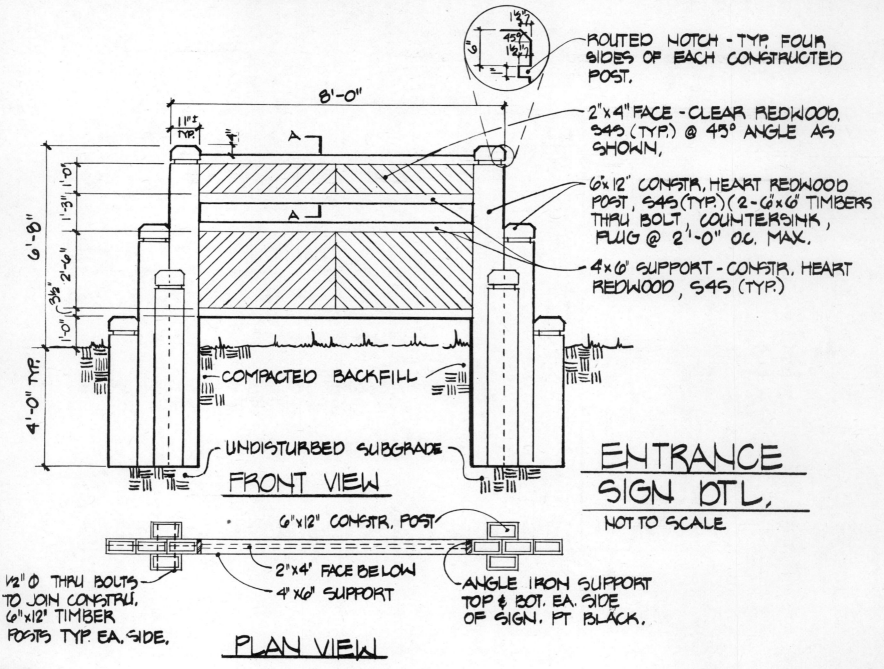

ROUTED NOTCH - TYP. FOUR SIDES OF EACH CONSTRUCTED POST.

2"x4" FACE - CLEAR REDWOOD, S4S (TYP.) @ 45° ANGLE AS SHOWN.

6"x12" CONSTR. HEART REDWOOD POST, S4S (TYP.) (2-6"x6" TIMBERS THRU BOLT, COUNTERSINK, PLUG @ 2'-0" O.C. MAX.

4x6" SUPPORT - CONSTR. HEART REDWOOD, S4S (TYP.)

8'-0"

1"± TYP.

6'-8"

1'-0" / 1'-3" / 2'-0" / 3½" / 1'-0"

4'-0" TYP.

COMPACTED BACKFILL

UNDISTURBED SUBGRADE

FRONT VIEW

ENTRANCE SIGN DTL.
NOT TO SCALE

6"x12" CONSTR. POST

2"x4" FACE BELOW

4"x6" SUPPORT

½"Ø THRU BOLTS TO JOIN CONSTR. 6"x12" TIMBER POSTS TYP. EA. SIDE.

ANGLE IRON SUPPORT TOP & BOT. EA. SIDE OF SIGN. PT BLACK.

PLAN VIEW

98

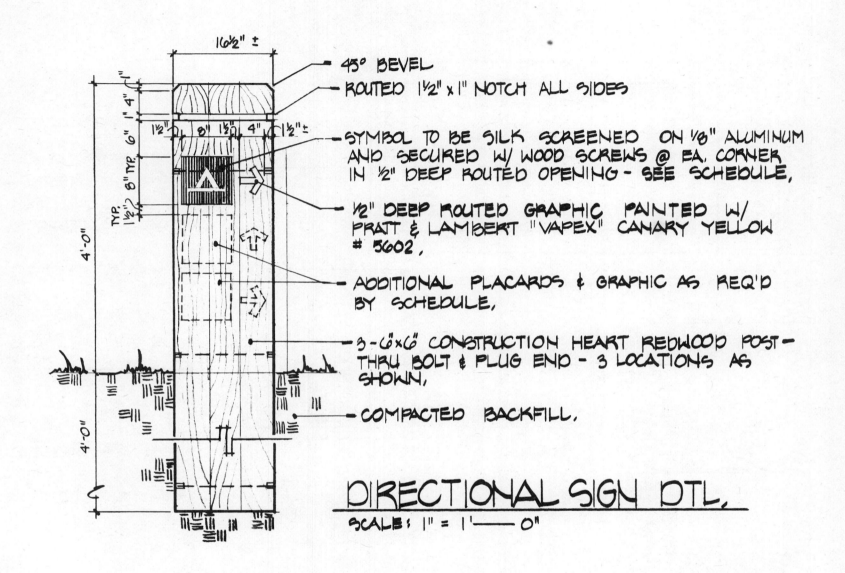

45° BEVEL

ROUTED 1½" x 1" NOTCH ALL SIDES

SYMBOL TO BE SILK SCREENED ON ⅛" ALUMINUM AND SECURED W/ WOOD SCREWS @ EA. CORNER IN ½" DEEP ROUTED OPENING - SEE SCHEDULE.

½" DEEP ROUTED GRAPHIC PAINTED W/ PRATT & LAMBERT "VAPEX" CANARY YELLOW # 5602.

ADDITIONAL PLACARDS & GRAPHIC AS REQ'D BY SCHEDULE.

3 - 6"x6" CONSTRUCTION HEART REDWOOD POST - THRU BOLT & PLUG END - 3 LOCATIONS AS SHOWN.

COMPACTED BACKFILL.

DIRECTIONAL SIGN DTL.

SCALE: 1" = 1'——0"

99

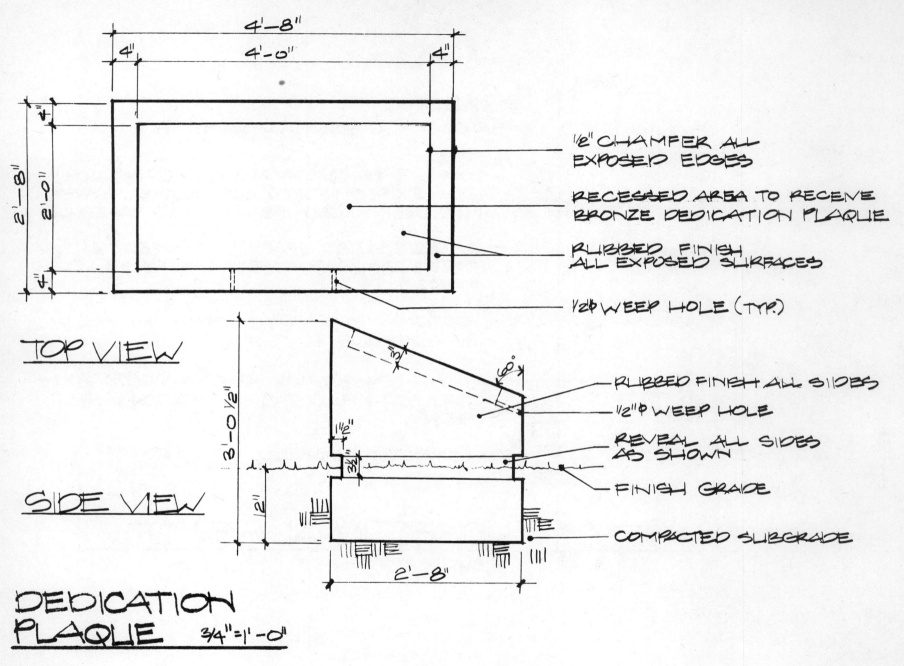

4'-8"

4'-0"

4"   4"

4"

2'-8"

2'-0"

4"

½" CHAMFER ALL
EXPOSED EDGES

RECESSED AREA TO RECEIVE
BRONZE DEDICATION PLAQUE

RUBBED FINISH
ALL EXPOSED SURFACES

½"⌀ WEEP HOLE (TYP.)

TOP VIEW

3"

8°

3'-0½"

1½"

3½"

12"

2'-8"

RUBBED FINISH ALL SIDES

½"⌀ WEEP HOLE

REVEAL ALL SIDES
AS SHOWN

FINISH GRADE

COMPACTED SUBGRADE

SIDE VIEW

DEDICATION
PLAQUE   ¾"=1'-0"

100

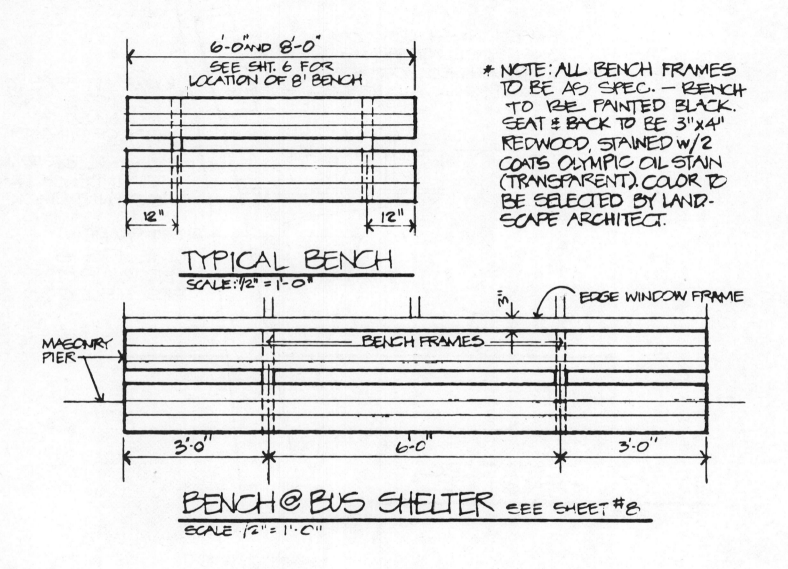

6'-0" AND 8'-0"
SEE SHT. 6 FOR
LOCATION OF 8' BENCH

12"   12"

TYPICAL BENCH
SCALE: 1/2" = 1'-0"

* NOTE: ALL BENCH FRAMES
TO BE AS SPEC. — BENCH
TO BE PAINTED BLACK.
SEAT & BACK TO BE 3"×4"
REDWOOD, STAINED w/2
COATS OLYMPIC OIL STAIN
(TRANSPARENT). COLOR TO
BE SELECTED BY LAND-
SCAPE ARCHITECT.

3"   EDGE WINDOW FRAME

MASONRY
PIER

BENCH FRAMES

3'-0"   6'-0"   3'-0"

BENCH @ BUS SHELTER SEE SHEET #8
SCALE 1/2" = 1'-0"

101

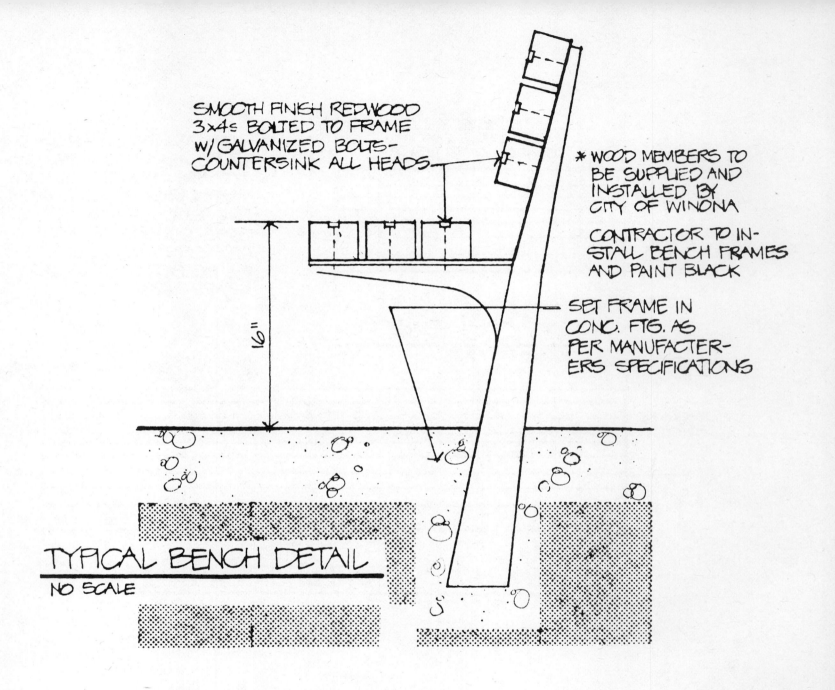

SMOOTH FINISH REDWOOD
3×4s BOLTED TO FRAME
W/ GALVANIZED BOLTS-
COUNTERSINK ALL HEADS

* WOOD MEMBERS TO
BE SUPPLIED AND
INSTALLED BY
CITY OF WINONA

CONTRACTOR TO IN-
STALL BENCH FRAMES
AND PAINT BLACK

SET FRAME IN
CONC. FTG. AS
PER MANUFACTER-
ERS SPECIFICATIONS

16"

TYPICAL BENCH DETAIL
NO SCALE

102

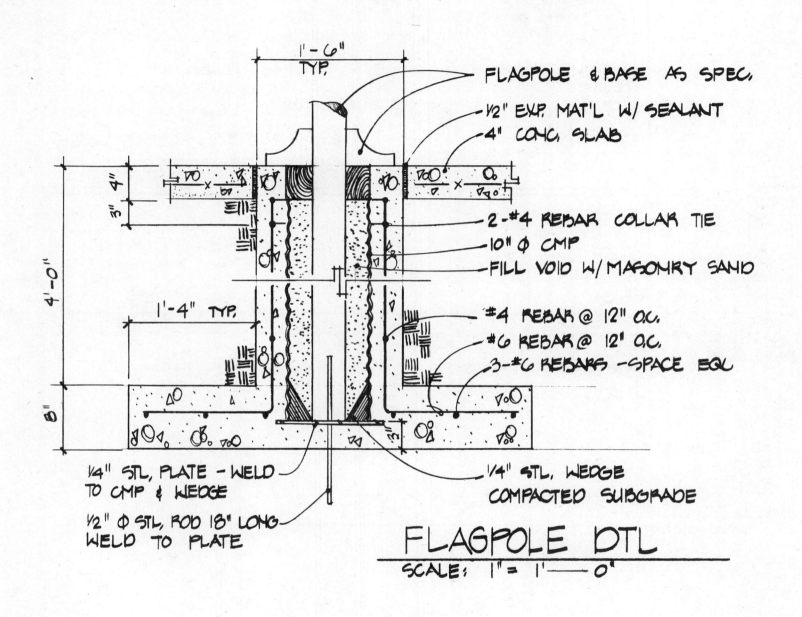

FLAGPOLE & BASE AS SPEC.

1/2" EXP. MAT'L W/ SEALANT

4" CONC. SLAB

2 - #4 REBAR COLLAR TIE

10" Ø CMP

FILL VOID W/ MASONRY SAND

#4 REBAR @ 12" O.C.

#6 REBAR @ 12" O.C.

3 - #6 REBARS - SPACE EQ

1/4" STL. WEDGE
COMPACTED SUBGRADE

1'-6"
TYP.

4'-0"

4"

3"

1'-4" TYP.

8"

1/4" STL. PLATE - WELD
TO CMP & WEDGE

1/2" Ø STL. ROD 18" LONG
WELD TO PLATE

FLAGPOLE DTL
SCALE: 1" = 1'——0"

103

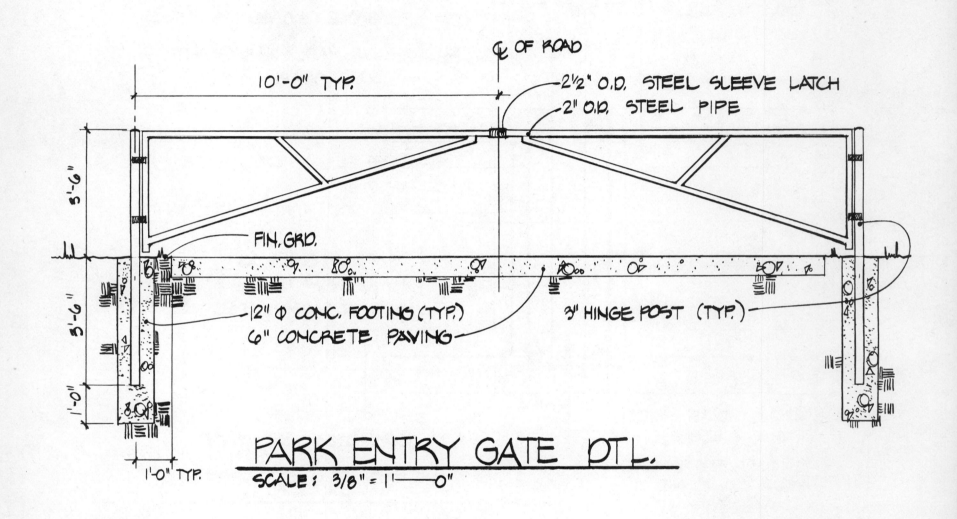

CL OF ROAD

10'-0" TYP.

2½" O.D. STEEL SLEEVE LATCH

2" O.D. STEEL PIPE

5'-6"

FIN. GRD.

5'-6"

12" Ø CONC. FOOTING (TYP.)

6" CONCRETE PAVING

3" HINGE POST (TYP.)

1'-0"

1'-0" TYP.

PARK ENTRY GATE DTL.
SCALE: 3/8" = 1'—0"

104

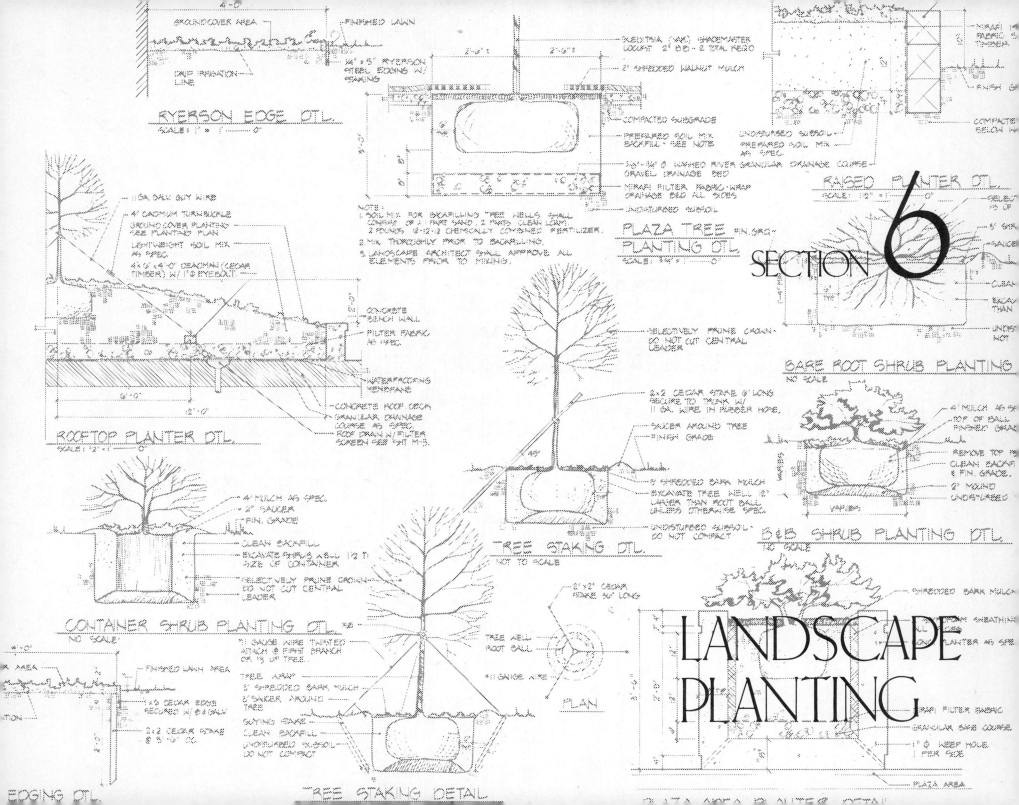

SECTION 6

LANDSCAPE PLANTING

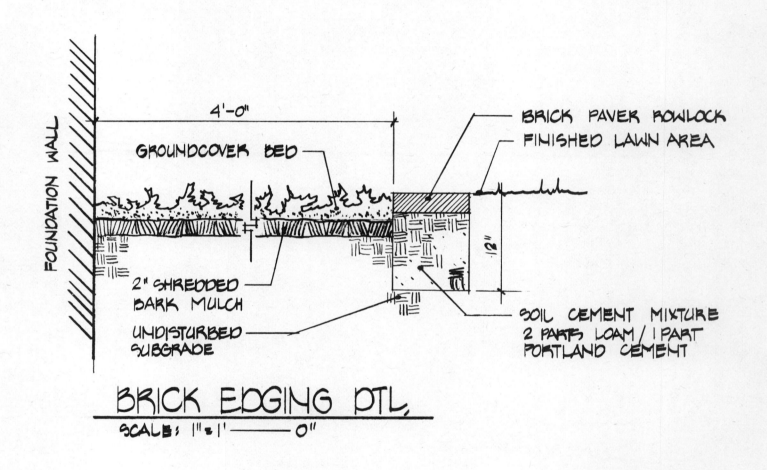

FOUNDATION WALL

4'-0"

GROUNDCOVER BED

BRICK PAVER ROWLOCK

FINISHED LAWN AREA

12"

2" SHREDDED BARK MULCH

UNDISTURBED SUBGRADE

SOIL CEMENT MIXTURE 2 PARTS LOAM / 1 PART PORTLAND CEMENT

BRICK EDGING DTL.

SCALE: 1" = 1' ——— 0"

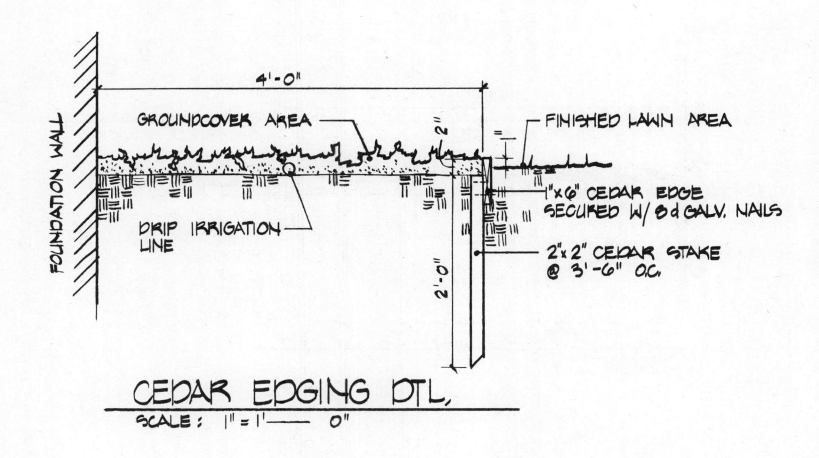

FOUNDATION WALL

4'-0"

GROUNDCOVER AREA

2"

FINISHED LAWN AREA

DRIP IRRIGATION LINE

1"x6" CEDAR EDGE SECURED W/ 8d GALV. NAILS

2'-0"

2"x2" CEDAR STAKE @ 3'-6" O.C.

CEDAR EDGING DTL.

SCALE: 1" = 1' —— 0"

107

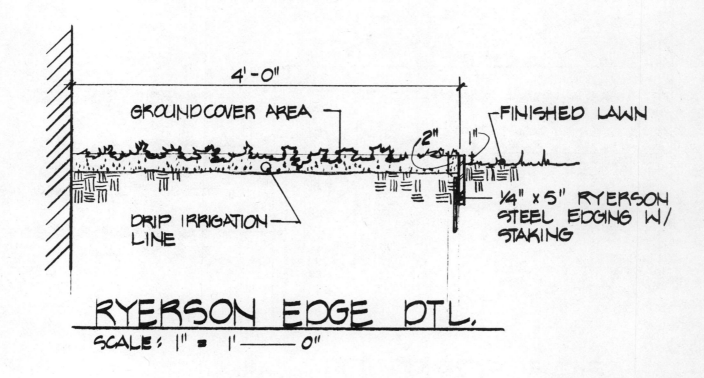

4'-0"

GROUNDCOVER AREA

FINISHED LAWN

2"

1"

DRIP IRRIGATION LINE

1/4" x 5" RYERSON STEEL EDGING W/ STAKING

RYERSON EDGE DTL.

SCALE: 1" = 1' —— 0"

108

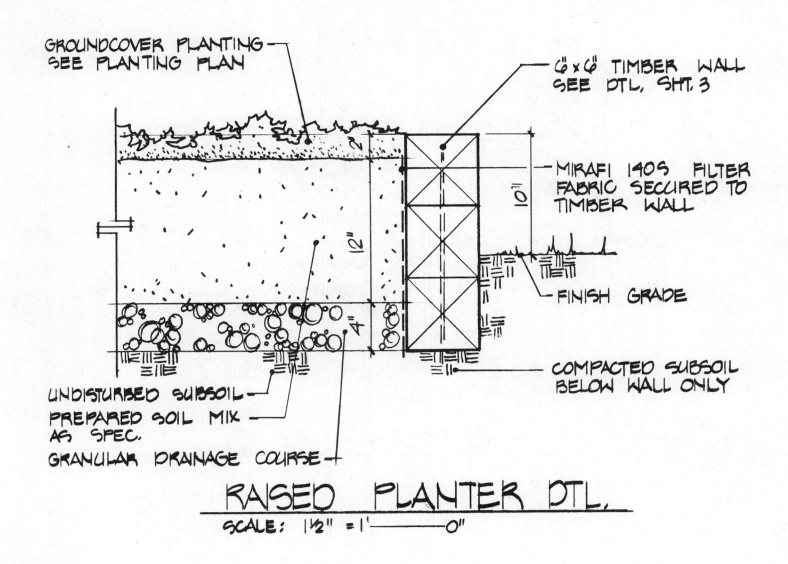

GROUNDCOVER PLANTING —
SEE PLANTING PLAN

6" x 6" TIMBER WALL
SEE DTL, SHT. 3

MIRAFI 140S FILTER
FABRIC SECURED TO
TIMBER WALL

FINISH GRADE

COMPACTED SUBSOIL
BELOW WALL ONLY

UNDISTURBED SUBSOIL
PREPARED SOIL MIX
AS SPEC.
GRANULAR DRAINAGE COURSE

12"

4"

2"

10"

RAISED PLANTER DTL.

SCALE: 1½" = 1' ———— 0"

109

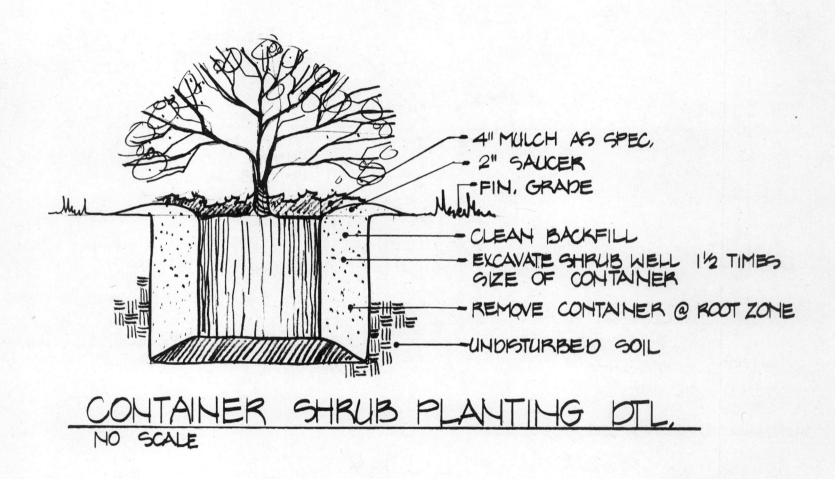

4" MULCH AS SPEC.

2" SAUCER

FIN. GRADE

CLEAN BACKFILL

EXCAVATE SHRUB WELL 1½ TIMES SIZE OF CONTAINER

REMOVE CONTAINER @ ROOT ZONE

UNDISTURBED SOIL

CONTAINER SHRUB PLANTING DTL.
NO SCALE

110

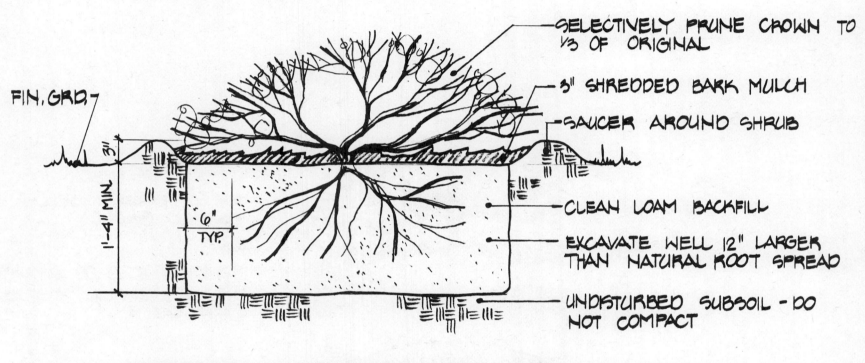

SELECTIVELY PRUNE CROWN TO ⅓ OF ORIGINAL

3" SHREDDED BARK MULCH

SAUCER AROUND SHRUB

FIN. GRD.

3"

1'-4" MIN.

6" TYP.

CLEAN LOAM BACKFILL

EXCAVATE WELL 12" LARGER THAN NATURAL ROOT SPREAD

UNDISTURBED SUBSOIL - DO NOT COMPACT

BARE ROOT SHRUB PLANTING DTL.

NO SCALE

111

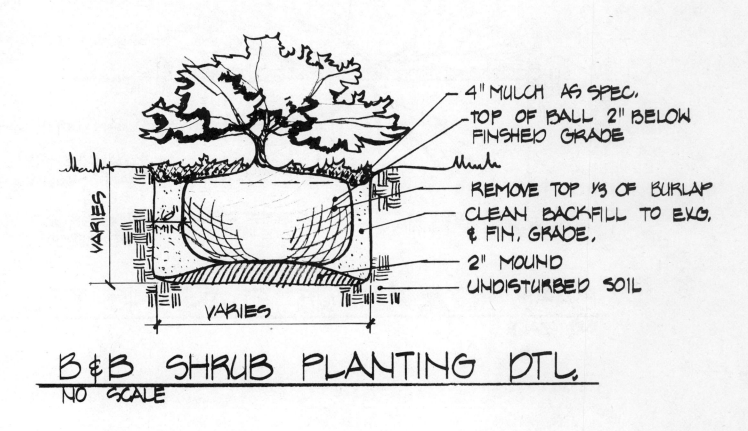

4" MULCH AS SPEC.

TOP OF BALL 2" BELOW FINSHED GRADE

REMOVE TOP 1/3 OF BURLAP

CLEAN BACKFILL TO EXG. & FIN. GRADE.

2" MOUND

UNDISTURBED SOIL

VARIES

VARIES

MIN

B & B SHRUB PLANTING DTL.

NO SCALE

112

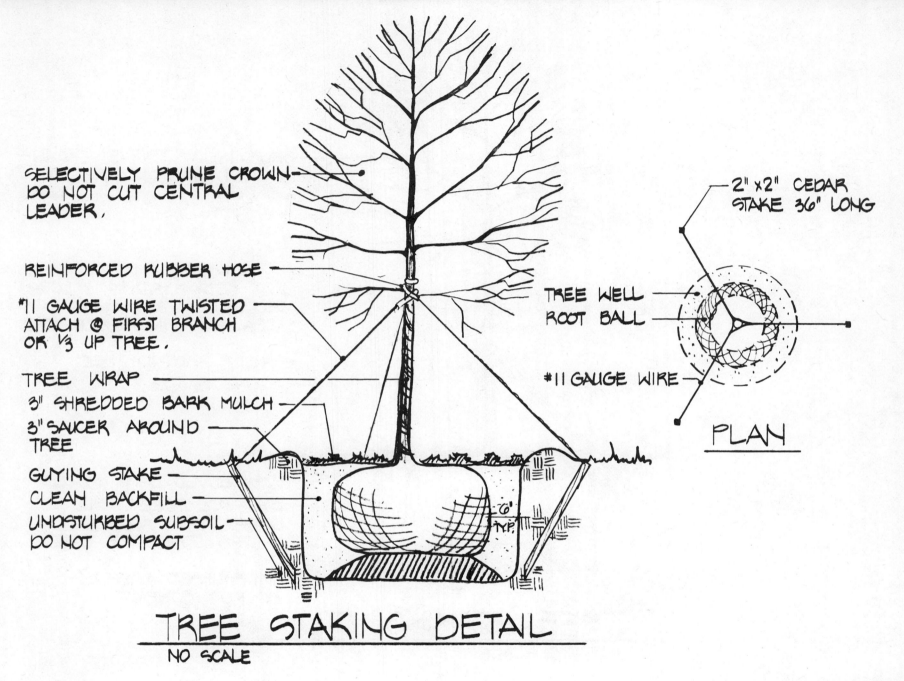

SELECTIVELY PRUNE CROWN-
DO NOT CUT CENTRAL
LEADER.

REINFORCED RUBBER HOSE

#11 GAUGE WIRE TWISTED
ATTACH @ FIRST BRANCH
OR ⅓ UP TREE.

TREE WRAP

3" SHREDDED BARK MULCH

3" SAUCER AROUND
TREE

GUYING STAKE

CLEAN BACKFILL

UNDISTURBED SUBSOIL-
DO NOT COMPACT

TREE WELL
ROOT BALL

#11 GAUGE WIRE

6'
TYP.

2" x 2" CEDAR
STAKE 36" LONG

PLAN

TREE STAKING DETAIL
NO SCALE

113

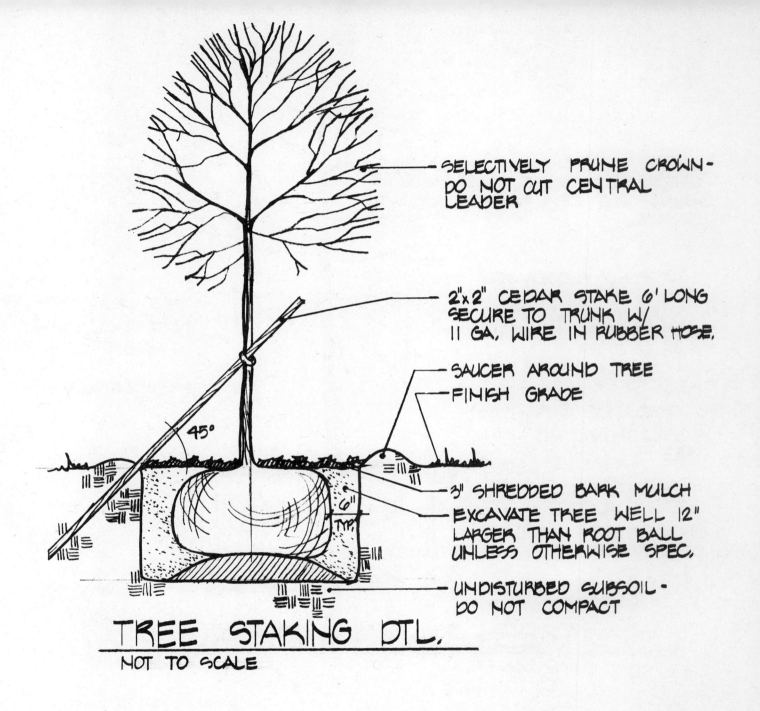

SELECTIVELY PRUNE CROWN-
DO NOT CUT CENTRAL
LEADER

2"x2" CEDAR STAKE 6' LONG
SECURE TO TRUNK W/
11 GA. WIRE IN RUBBER HOSE.

SAUCER AROUND TREE

FINISH GRADE

45°

3" SHREDDED BARK MULCH

EXCAVATE TREE WELL 12"
LARGER THAN ROOT BALL
UNLESS OTHERWISE SPEC.

UNDISTURBED SUBSOIL-
DO NOT COMPACT

6"
TYP.

TREE STAKING DTL.
NOT TO SCALE

114

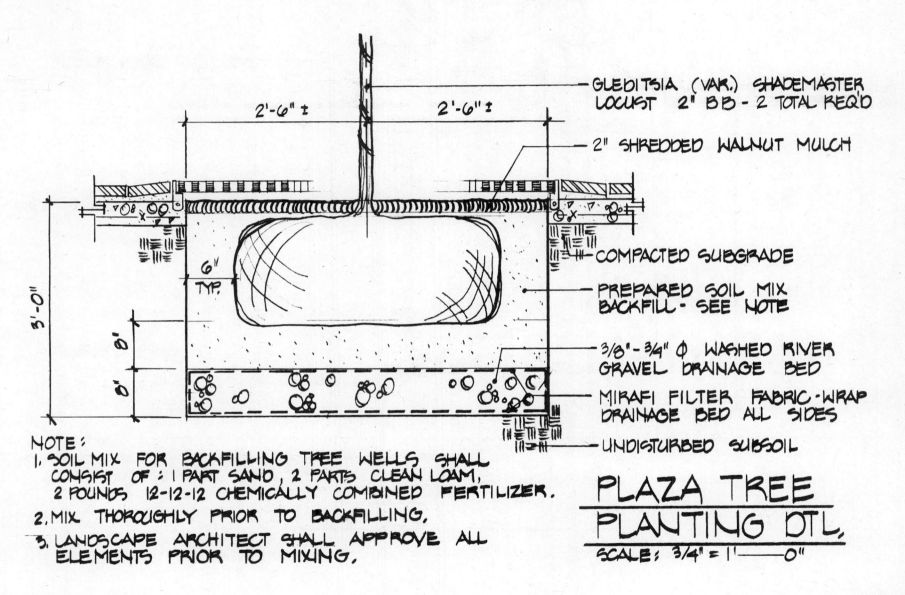

GLEDITSIA (VAR.) SHADEMASTER LOCUST 2" BB - 2 TOTAL REQ'D

2" SHREDDED WALNUT MULCH

COMPACTED SUBGRADE

PREPARED SOIL MIX BACKFILL - SEE NOTE

3/8" - 3/4" Ø WASHED RIVER GRAVEL DRAINAGE BED

MIRAFI FILTER FABRIC - WRAP DRAINAGE BED ALL SIDES

UNDISTURBED SUBSOIL

2'-6" ±   2'-6" ±

3'-0"

6" TYP.

8"

6"

NOTE:
1. SOIL MIX FOR BACKFILLING TREE WELLS SHALL CONSIST OF : 1 PART SAND, 2 PARTS CLEAN LOAM, 2 POUNDS 12-12-12 CHEMICALLY COMBINED FERTILIZER.

2. MIX THOROUGHLY PRIOR TO BACKFILLING.

3. LANDSCAPE ARCHITECT SHALL APPROVE ALL ELEMENTS PRIOR TO MIXING.

PLAZA TREE PLANTING DTL.
SCALE: 3/4" = 1'——0"

115

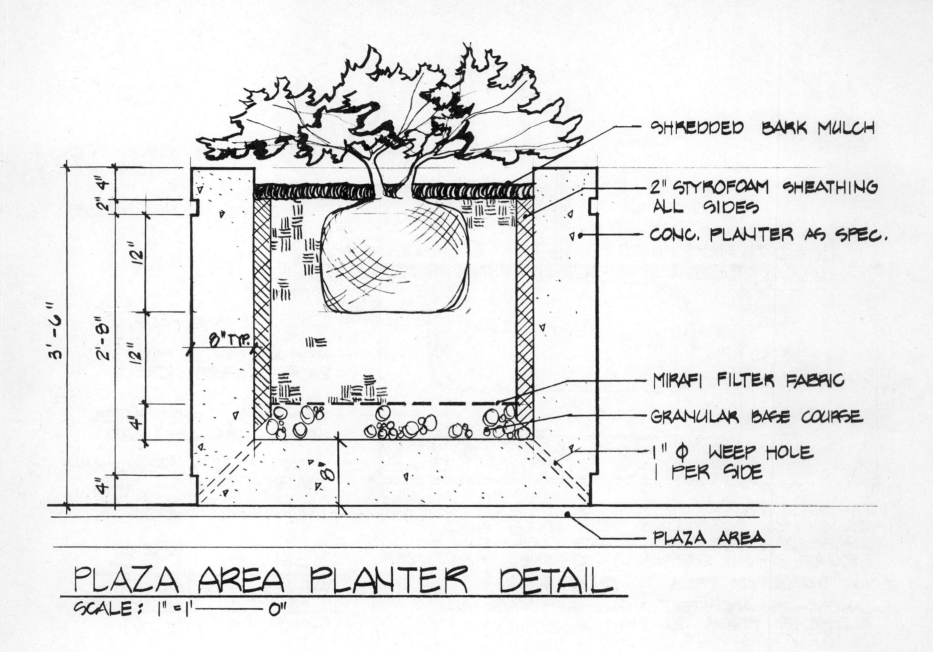

SHREDDED BARK MULCH

2" STYROFOAM SHEATHING
ALL SIDES

CONC. PLANTER AS SPEC.

MIRAFI FILTER FABRIC

GRANULAR BASE COURSE

1" Ø WEEP HOLE
1 PER SIDE

PLAZA AREA

3'-6"

2'-8"

4"

12"

12"

4"

4"

8" TYP.

8"

PLAZA AREA PLANTER DETAIL

SCALE: 1"=1'———0"

116

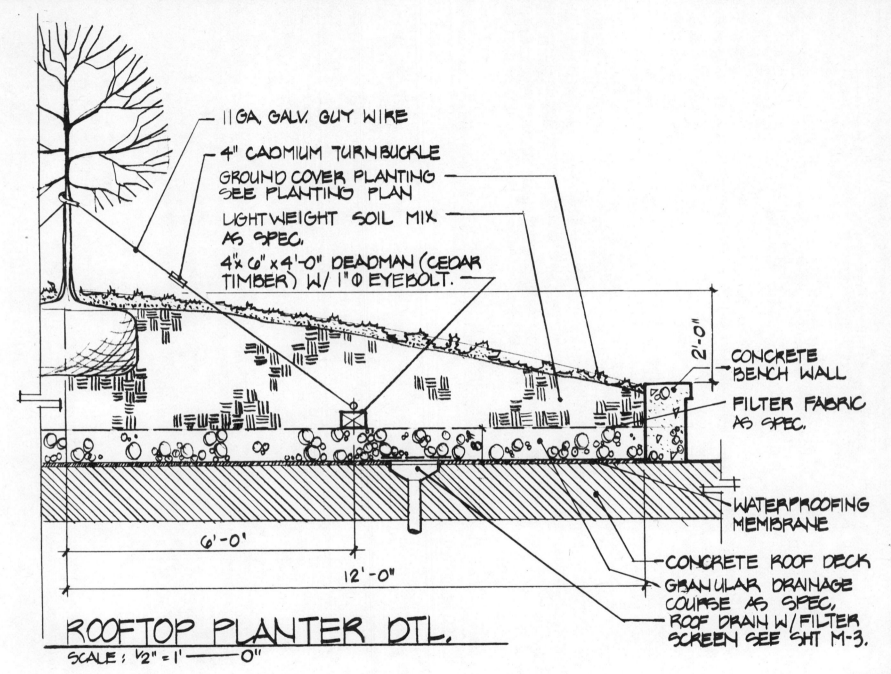

ROOFTOP PLANTER DTL.

SCALE: ½" = 1'—0"

11 GA. GALV. GUY WIRE

4" CADMIUM TURNBUCKLE

GROUND COVER PLANTING
SEE PLANTING PLAN

LIGHTWEIGHT SOIL MIX
AS SPEC.

4" × 6" × 4'-0" DEADMAN (CEDAR
TIMBER) W/ 1"Ø EYEBOLT.

CONCRETE
BENCH WALL

FILTER FABRIC
AS SPEC.

WATERPROOFING
MEMBRANE

CONCRETE ROOF DECK

GRANULAR DRAINAGE
COURSE AS SPEC.

ROOF DRAIN W/ FILTER
SCREEN SEE SHT M-3.

2'-0"

6'-0"

12'-0"

117

INDEX